Memoirs
of the Flight Surgeon
# of HMS Nabob

BY

Charles Herbert Read Jr.
MDCM
Surgeon Lieutenant RCNVR (R)

Lammi
Publishing Inc.

Published by Lammi Publishing, Inc., headquartered in Coaldale, Alberta, Canada.
http://lammipublishing.ca

This book is a memoir. The conversations in it were not recorded, but were reconstructed from the author's memory.

Text editing by Karen Hann

Cover design by Paul Hewitt, Battlefield Design

Library and Archives Canada Cataloguing in Publication

Read, Charles H., Jr., 1918-2016, author
   Memoirs of the flight surgeon of HMS Nabob/by Charles Herbert Read Jr.

Issued in print and electronic formats.
ISBN 978-0-9950060-8-9 (softcover)
ISBN 978-0-9950060-7-2 (Amazon Kindle)
ISBN 978-0-9950060-6-5 (EPUB)

1. Read, Charles H., Jr., 1918-2016. 2. Nabob (Aircraft carrier). 3. Great Britain. Royal Navy—Surgeons—Biography. 4. World War, 1939-1945—Personal narratives, Canadian. 5. World War, 1939-1945—Naval operations, Canadian. 6. Canada—History, Naval—20th century. 7. Great Britain—History, Naval—20th century. I. Title.

D772.N3R43 2017   359.3'2550941   C2017-903321-2

C2017-903322-0

To all the men and women who fought Hitler and his Nazis, especially to those brave men who served on the HMS Nabob.

Table of Contents

Chapter One

An Odd Name for an Aircraft Carrier

The rocky peninsula of Halifax is partially surrounded by one of the most coveted features of a northern coastal settlement—an ice-free harbour. The Halifax Harbour has been vital to Canada's defense and development throughout our birth and early growth as a nation.

The British Empire created a military outpost in this harbour in 1749. The Royal British Navy established the first dockyard there, and the facility has grown and expanded ever since, passing into Canadian control in the early 1900s. It underwent massive expansion during the First World War, only to be severely damaged in the infamous Halifax explosion of 1917 and then quickly rebuilt. These dockyards are also the site of the legendary Pier 21, where over a million immigrants entered Canada, weaving in their own colours and patterns into the fabric of this nation. Today, it remains a commercial port, a tourist site, and a military stronghold.

At the North End of the Halifax Peninsula, the British Army built the Wellington Barracks in 1797. The site of these barracks eventually moved into Canadian hands, and at the onset of the Second World War it was appropriated by the Canadian Navy and transformed into the facility known as HMCS Stadacona. Such historical Canadian landmarks as Wellington Gate and Admiralty House remain standing there to this day.

It was there that I, as a new medical officer in the Royal Canadian Navy, reported on 3 January, 1944. The Officer of the Day at once told me I was to report to Surgeon Lieutenant Commander Neil Chapman in the outpatient clinic in the dockyards. After a relatively short walk, I found him standing in the door of his office, holding a piece of paper. I thought he looked like someone who had just been surprised. Then he saw me. After welcoming me, he told me that he had received a cable

1

from headquarters in Ottawa, telling him the wonderful news that the Canadian Navy had just acquired an aircraft carrier. He showed me the document.

Chapman was obviously excited. Now that our navy had an aircraft carrier, we really had it all. During the First World War, Canada had been a British dominion, subject to the decisions of the British Parliament. We'd proved our mettle as a nation then, fighting such legendary battles as the Somme, Vimy, and Passchendaele. Now, thanks to the Statute of Westminster, we were a fully sovereign nation, able to make our military decisions independently. Of course, as responsible citizens of the world who were horrified at the atrocities of Hitler, we had joined the Allied war effort. In the First World War, aircraft carrier technology had been rudimentary, but the inter-war years had brought about innovations allowing for far more effective, large-scale use of the vessels. Aircraft carriers allow naval forces to project air power great distances without having to depend on local staging bases, a true union of air and sea warfare.

This news was also tremendously exciting to me. Up until now, being a physician in the Canadian Navy had meant to me that in due course, I would probably get to go to sea on a corvette, frigate, or maybe even a destroyer, and I would see new places and have many new experiences. Furthermore, I'd be involved in any action and share the same risks as the rest of the crew. But now, this joining of the air and the sea at once seemed to me to be a whole new and ideal way to fight the anti-submarine war. Immediately, I decided I wanted to be the flight surgeon on that aircraft carrier, because it would epitomize the way I could best contribute to the war effort and Hitler's defeat. In that role, I thought I'd be attending to the special needs of the aircrew as well as the general medical needs of the others of the crew.

But over the next few hours, when I thought about my chances of getting that appointment, it struck me that they were virtually zero. I spent time at the legendary Admiralty House, where I learned more. Admiralty House had once been the official residence of the admiral of the North American Station of the British Royal Navy, housing such famous residents as Admiral Thomas Cochrane, Earl of Dundonald, and Admiral Francis Austen, brother of Jane Austen. After it passed into Canadian hands, it served as a naval hospital in the First World

War (sustaining heavy damage in the Halifax explosion), and now, in the Second World War, as an officer's club. I had no seniority, and from listening to the lunchtime chatter, it was evident that virtually all the fifty or so other medical officers at Admiralty House (then the Naval Officer's Club in Halifax) all wanted it. And that was not considering the three hundred and more doctors elsewhere in the navy, all of whom had more seniority than I, and all of whom probably wanted that position as much as I did.

I needed to find a way to set myself apart and increase my chances.

The only thing I could do was to make it known that I wanted that appointment; the worse that could happen then would be that I would be ignored or told no. That very afternoon, I found out that the most senior medical officer at Stadacona was Surgeon Captain David Johnston, and therefore, I naively presumed, the person who would make the decision.

I made an appointment to see him as soon as I could. It turned out to be the next afternoon.

So when I knocked on his door, I made sure I was precisely on time. A pleasant voice invited me in. He was alone. As he rose to greet me, I saw he was of medium height, and other than having four wavy gold rings separated by scarlet ones on both sleeves, he looked much like the kindly, middle-aged physician he'd probably been before volunteering for the service. The warmth of his personality and the tone of his voice put me more at ease, but I was careful to stand at attention with my cap properly tucked under my left arm. He invited me to have a seat and did so himself, asking how he could help me.

My statement was brief. I told him that I was aware we'd just acquired the aircraft carrier, and I would dearly love to be a medical officer aboard the ship. I hoped that when the time came to assign someone, he might consider me.

He looked at me intently, as if he was wondering what kind of a person I might be, but otherwise the expression on his face did not change. He simply got to his feet, as did I, and slowly walked me to the door.

He thanked me for coming to tell him this.

That was all; he didn't even ask me a question. The meeting had lasted maybe a minute. I went back to my office in the dockyards and began seeing patients. I presumed it would be some time before I'd hear anything.

In the time I'd been working in the clinic, I'd found the three other medical officers and the non-commissioned officers both proficient and pleasant. The office hours were 0900-1700, and we four doctors rotated night call every fourth day. Our patients were able-bodied seamen and non-commissioned officers, all of whom had volunteered for the service. When a medical problem was difficult, consultations with well-qualified physicians and surgeons were immediately available at the nearby Naval Hospital. If hospitalization was appropriate, admission was prompt. I thought it was a great way to practice medicine.

Most nights were surprisingly routine, considering the fact that 60,000 service men and women were living in the city and on the ships in the harbour and, I was told, were dependent on us. But one night early in January was quite unusual. About 0200, a signal from an American LST (Landing Ship Tank) anchored in Bedford Basin (a major extension of Halifax Harbour where trans-Atlantic convoys were organized) said they had a sailor complaining of abdominal pain. They suspected appendicitis. It was my responsibility to ascertain if this was accurate. Boarding a launch, I had an enjoyable five-mile trip on a calm sea under a clear, crisp, mid-January sky filled with stars and illuminated by a full moon. The ship, the USS Roger Williams, was anchored amongst almost a hundred other ships. In their Sick Bay, I took a careful history and conducted a complete physical examination. As the patient had no signs of appendicitis or other organic disease, I concluded that his symptoms were mostly (consciously or sub-consciously) due to an acute attack of not wanting to cross the Atlantic Ocean. I gave a copy of my report to the executive officer and kept one for my own records.

In those weeks, I saw the Surgeon Captain frequently at Admiralty House. Invariably, he was surrounded by one or more medical officers, all of whom seemed to want to make sure he did not lack for drink. Occasionally, I heard snatches of conversation; often, it was about the new aircraft carrier. That is how I learned its name: HMS Nabob. To me, it seemed a strange name for a warship. Surely it wasn't named after an Indian potentate. Even less appropriate, I thought, would be if it were named after a brand of tea popular in Canada. And why was it not designated HMCS, if it really was a Canadian ship? I felt it prudent to keep such observations to myself.

On two different occasions, I had to inspect Flower-class corvettes that the Royal Navy

used as anti-submarine escorts for convoys. They were generally equipped with both minesweeping and anti-aircraft capabilities, and would be vital for safe transport of our Canadian ships across the Atlantic. Upon inspecting these ships, I found that the sinks, showers and other facilities in the heads (navy term for toilets) were utterly filthy. I ordered that they had to be replaced before I would accept the ships. I was especially vigilant, because I'd heard well-founded rumors that the British were modernizing their own ships, but not ours (later substantiated) as they had agreed to. Apparently, the Royal Navy still had great difficulty remembering we Canadians were not a part of their navy, nor were we colonials to be treated as they wished. I was on the look-out for this, because when I was a teenager I had read two detailed, twenty-volume histories of what went on in the First World War. A few days later, I found that the problems had been resolved as I'd ordered, and there were new and clean head facilities on board the corvettes. I was surprised at how much power the insignia on my sleeves, two wavy gold stripes with a red one between, apparently gave me.

Another odd job I had on several occasions was conducting tours for VIPs who wanted to visit our facilities. I hardly knew more about our ships than which end was the bow and which the stern, but I managed to conceal my ignorance as I took each visitor to the designated ship and introduced them to the Officer of the Day, saying, "Please tell the captain he has a guest." I assumed the captain would have his steward set up an adequate supply of liquor and would introduce the guest to the officers who were available. This procedure seemed satisfactory. The guests invariably stayed quite some time, because drinking duty-free liquor on board a warship was quite the treat. I often wondered how the American Navy, said to have no liquor in their wardrooms, coped with visitors.

On another afternoon, I was invited to watch a corvette crew in action, a part of a unique refresher course developed in 1942 by

Commander Hibbard, a veteran of many nighttime sea actions. Held in a totally blacked-out large building, this particular exercise was a simulated night attack on a submerged submarine. After I dark-adapted, I recognized that I was on a replica of a bridge of a corvette, assigned to a spot where I was out of everyone's way but able to look both forward and aft. I heard the increasing pings of the sonar as we closed in on the supposed target and heard the commands of the officers to the crews manning the depth charges. It seemed very authentic, especially when the depth charges were released, and the sounds of the simulated explosions echoed through the building. I thought that this must be a very experienced crew, for they handled every situation so well. Later I found out that this was a unique action simulation program that other navies widely copied.

Having only officers as patients and thus a much lighter clinical load than before, I was able to accept an invitation for a speed trial of the HMCS Athabaskan, a Tribal-class destroyer. This heavily-armed vessel had been built for relatively short trips at high speeds in the North Atlantic. *Thrilled* would perhaps best describe my feelings as the ship left the jetty and then *pretty smart* when I found a spot on the wing of the bridge out of everyone's way. I still had a wide breadth of vision, but I was so fixated on what lay immediately ahead that any ships in the harbour were but a blur. I do remember passing McNab's Island on our port side and then heading for the guard ships with their anti-submarine nets that protected the Halifax Harbour. Once we passed these nets, we were loose in the open Atlantic. I could feel the ship building speed as she sliced through the long ocean roll. Quickly, she reached full speed and the land, so recently left behind, soon disappeared. She was as I had imagined—a greyhound of the sea, but armed and ready to deliver more than just a bite. My only disappoint-ment was that the trip didn't last long enough. Apparently, whatever was being tested was found to be okay; this happened too quickly for my taste.

The HMCS Athabascan ended up having a short, but glorious life. She escorted convoys to the Soviet Union and then participated in both Operation Hostile, a minelaying operation, and Operation Tunnel, a patrol mission, off the coast of France before being sunk in the English

Channel by German torpedo boats in April of 1944, taking many of her crew down with her.

The inter-war years had not brought the same prosperity and growth to the Halifax region that they had to other areas of Canada. The city's position as an Allied staging area during the Second World War brought in a sudden influx of population and business, and it had become advantageous for local residents to open their homes to boarders, usually military personnel who didn't live on base. My wife Anne and I found a place in Bedford, a town just outside of the city, with a family called DeWolfe. Mr. DeWolfe was kind enough to ensure my transportation to and from the dockyards.

The day after my adventure on the ill-fated HMCS Athabascan was 27 February, and twenty inches of snow fell, large white flakes that slowly erased all the drabness that characterized wartime Halifax. When I awoke the next morning, the ground had an unblemished white cover that shimmered in the brightness of the morning sun. That morning, I discussed with Mr. DeWolfe whether the trip to the dockyards would be difficult due to the snow. But to our surprise, the road crews had been to work early and had done their work well. In the city, the streets were a mess, but as the sidewalks had been plowed, the walk down to the dockyard from Admiralty House was not difficult.

I'd hardly had a chance to take off my coat when the Chief Petty Officer (CPO) appeared at my door. "Sir," his voice a little higher than usual, he looked as if he were bursting with excitement. This was not at all the composed, totally in control man with whom I was used to working. "Sir," he repeated, "Dr. Chapman would like to see you right away."

I wondered why in the world Neil would want to talk to me with such urgency and why the CPO (Chief Petty Officer) was so excited. Neil's door was open and as soon as I arrived at the door, he got up to meet me and then blurted out, "Charlie, you are to report to H.M.S. Nabob in Norfolk, Virginia on 10 March. Congratulations." He shook my hand vigorously and said a few more things, too, instructions and whatnots, but they didn't matter. I'd heard all I needed to know. The unbelievable had happened. I was going to Nabob! I'd been chosen from all the others, even though I'd been in the Navy for only three months (one at HMCS Queen Charlotte in Charlottetown and now two at HMCS Stadacona) and had no seniority! The skin on the top of my head tingled. I knew what that was; an adrenaline rush. It was like a Christmas present such as I'd never had before.

All the staff seemed pleased for me. They helped me pack my things together and saw that I had my travel orders and other such documents. I wondered if the promotion to Officers Medical officer and all the little jobs I'd done in the last month were a part of a testing process. I didn't know, nor would I ever find out, but that didn't matter. The important thing was that I was going to be a medical officer (maybe a flight surgeon) on Nabob, the first Canadian-manned aircraft carrier.

When I returned to Bedford with Mr. De Wolfe and told Anne, she hugged me and told me how wonderful it was, how pleased I must be, and how amazing it was that I'd gotten the position. As this would mean I would soon be absent, I suspected that she wasn't quite as enthusiastic as she seemed, but Anne was a loyal wife and I appreciated her support. She didn't say much more, but she certainly fully co-operated and acted as if she were happy about it. Countless other women in Canada were in those same shoes, saying good-bye to their husbands, wishing them well as they went out into the world to fight the evil that was Nazism, not knowing if they would return.

After more than these four long years of preparation for this role, but only two months as a doctor in Stadacona, suddenly I was going to be actually actively involved in the war against Hitler. It was surreal, but wonderful. I was on my way!

Chapter Two

Fifteen Cents for Rum and Coke

On 9 March, I said good-bye to Anne in Montreal, where she would remain while I went overseas. I boarded a train for my journey to join Nabob in Norfolk, Virginia, via New York City. Seated comfortably in the parlor car, I had time to reflect upon the course my life had taken since Labor Day, 3 September, 1939. I'd been standing at the corner of Peel and St. Catherine St. in Montreal when I saw the headlines in the Montreal Star and the Montreal Gazette in a newspaper kiosk. In huge print, they'd said it all: "NAZI HORDES CRUSH POLAND" and "BRITAIN AND FRANCE DECLARE WAR ON GERMANY." As I normally kept up with the news, I was not surprised at the words. As soon as our Parliament met, Canada would be in the war. I resolved that I would be as well, for I understood the evil of Nazi philosophy and I wanted to be involved in the effort to defeat Hitler.

During my just completed college years, I'd read Hitler's *Mein Kampf* and read the reports of his aggressive actions in Europe during the past several years. I saw that he'd carried out his schemes, one after another, just as he'd described them in his book. To me, it was obvious that not only was he a major threat to all of Europe, but also to our Canadian way of life. Defeating this man, his philosophy, and his armed forces was an imperative and I was determined to have a role in it. Being twenty-one years old, a prime age for military service, I wondered if I should join one of our military services right away, and if so, which one?

But then I remembered why I was in Montreal. I'd been accepted as a student by the McGill University Medical School, where classes were to begin the very next day. So the question became, whether I joined up immediately or went to medical school as I'd planned. I debated this back and forth until finally I decided to postpone my decision until I'd heard what might be said at our class meeting scheduled for the next morning.

At eight o'clock the next morning, I was waiting in the main lecture room of the Medical Building with the rest of my new classmates, fifty-five of whom were Canadians, forty-five of whom were Americans. A vivacious, alert, and attractive brunette who introduced herself as Barbara Brooks pointed out to me important persons such as the secretary of the medical school who apparently ran the place; Dr. Walter Penfield, a neat-looking man who was a famous neurosurgeon, and Dr. Simpson, the dean.

Dr. Simpson welcomed us, but it was Dr. Penfield who talked about the question I was considering. He came across as a warm and caring individual, and his comments confirmed that for me. "I have a special word for those of you who are Canadians," he said. "With the war on against Nazi Germany, which Canada will probably soon join, you may be wondering, should you begin medical school now or should you enlist in one of the armed services. I say to you, without question, that you will make a much greater contribution to Canada's war effort as a doctor than you could in any other way. This is not going to be a short war and I'm sure you'll all be in it before it's over."

Those words, burned into my mind, made the decision.

Four years and a few months later, I graduated. In late January of 1943, I began a rotating internship at The Royal Victoria Hospital in Montreal. Now, I thought, I was really on my way to getting into this war. However, there were still eleven months to go with patients. Every day, I maintained a close relationship with my teaching physicians and my night and day responsibilities were both intensely interesting and absolutely critical in furthering my medical education.

My first rotation was on a very active thirty-five bed pediatric ward, which meant it began with a bang. I soon realized that children were not just small adults and required learning how to cope with their unique problems. Only a few weeks after I started, my supervising resident physician left to join the U.S. Army and no replacement came. Working alone meant there was no time for sleep or even any rest. Being coherent when making rounds each day with my supervising professors became increasingly difficult. I began to struggle to remember each patient's problems. Finally, at the end of five days without sleep, I developed a fever of one hundred and five degrees and became a patient myself. Diagnosis: exhaustion. After a twenty-four-hour sleep, all was well and I resumed my duties, but now I had the help of another intern.

Next, I rotated for three months in general surgery. Although this was not an area I wanted to pursue in depth, I enjoyed assisting in a large number of operations. After about a dozen appendectomies, I was given the role of chief surgeon for one, which proved to be a very useful experience. The plastic surgeon, Dr. Happy Baxter, showed me how to repair a laceration so that there would be little or no scar. However, overall, I was very disappointed with the surgery rotation, because we had little acute trauma to cope with because few accident victims arrived at our hospital.

One quiet Sunday evening when I was on Ear, Nose and Throat, my last rotation, I had time to have an extended conversation with one of my recovering patients, Marjorie Wallace, a Women's Auxiliary Air Force (WAAF) officer. When, at last, I told her that I would soon be leaving to join the military, she insisted on giving me her parents' address in Edinburgh, 102 Ravelstone Dykes. "Who knows," she said, "maybe you'll be there someday."

Edinburgh, I thought. *I suppose it's possible, but not very likely.*

Soon after, I had to make a final decision about which service I would join. My first inclination had been the Royal Canadian Air Force, but upon enquiring I learned that many of the Air Force medical officers were posted to places in Canada; places far removed from the field of action. I was told that others dispatched to RCAF units in the United Kingdom often remained in the same posting for prolonged periods. This was not what I wanted. I wanted to be in the middle of the action, making what I felt was a real contribution to Nazism's defeat.

In contrast, the Navy had a rotation that involved working in an out-patient service, at a naval base or on a ship at sea, followed by a refresher period in a major civilian hospital or at a recruiting base, where it was important for the examiner to know whether a recruit's medical problem would preclude his activities in the service. I also learned that their recruits were from the top ten per cent of their medical class. Thankfully, I qualified. That might help me be selected.

However, the real attraction was the possibility that I might serve at sea, where I would share the same risks as the rest of the crew. This appealed to me greatly, for I would feel more like I was fighting Hitler. I remembered reading a book when I was very young called *Airmen O' War*, in which the Royal Flying Corp pilots in France during the First World War, said of their lives that "they lived like gentlemen, fought like gentlemen and died like gentlemen." I thought this might be true for the navy as well. So I applied the next day. Two days later, I received a letter of acceptance. I could hardly believe the quickness of the response. I was in the Navy. My full title was Surgeon Lieutenant Charles H. Read Jr., Royal Canadian Navy Volunteer Reserve. I was to report to HMCS Stadacona in Halifax, Nova Scotia. At last, I was going to actually participate in the fight!

In contrast to the comfortable, day-long trip in a parlor car to New York, the overnight trip in a coach to Norfolk was hot, crowded, and smelled of orange peels and cigarette smoke. That, coupled with the jolting of the train, made most of the journey very unpleasant. However, because of that, I was still awake when we came to the long bridge crossing Chesapeake Bay. That's when I saw the spectacular pre-dawn sky shine as the sun lit up the overhead clouds, eventually emerging from the sea as a fiery red ball; one stunning vista following another. I watched, spellbound. This was, I decided, undoubtedly a natural extravaganza, celebrating the beginning of my career on the Nabob.

I had no doubt about where I was when I arrived at the Norfolk Naval Base. The immediate and pervasive smell of diesel-oil exhaust and the pulsating rhythm that went on and on without pause, all day and all night, revealed the power and intensity of the activity taking place. The United States of America was at war; of that there was no doubt. I could see it even in the way everyone walked, intense and purposeful; no one sauntered. They talked the same way. Not a minute to lose. We benefitted from this super activity for, after a few days, Nabob went into dry dock at eight in the evening and emerged at six the next morning with a new, less noisy propeller, her bottom scraped and painted. Efficiency was in; wasting time was not.

However, when I first saw the HMS Nabob, I was shocked and disappointed. None of the sleek lines of the fleet carriers I'd seen in photographs were present. As a matter of fact, she hardly looked like a warship ship at all, but rather like a newly built Woolworth freighter or maybe just a rectangular box with a flat lid. I did not see any funnels or masts like most ships had. And what was that odd little house perched on its starboard (right) side with posts sticking out with attached wires? But then I saw boldly inscribed on her bow, the numeral 77. Those, I knew, were lucky numbers; somehow she would survive whatever evil came to her. That settled it for me. There she was, not very glamorous, but she was to be my ship and I was immediately excited to be one of her crew. As far as I was concerned, she was just fine.

I entered my ship through an opening in her port side and reported to the Officer of the Day. One of the two seamen carrying my trunk said my cabin was mid-ships and thwart-ships. This was lucky, he explained, because it meant I was right in the middle of the ship in both directions where there was the least amount of movement. I wouldn't get seasick.

I looked my new home over. Modest in size, it had two bunk beds on the left side, one above the other. I chose the lower and the men slipped my old cabin trunk under it. Opposite were two small individual desks and chairs, each complete with drawers and a sink, topped by a mirrored cabinet. Two identical closets were large enough for hanging uniforms and greatcoats. A fire-proof curtain hung in the door. I was satisfied.

After I thanked my helpers, I decided to explore the ship. Knowing that the wardroom would be the center for socializing, as well as where we would eat and drink, I decided that it would be a good place to start.

One of the seamen had said that it was just a short distance aft down the companionway. Being only about ten thirty in the morning, the only person there was Harold Chizy, the wardroom wine steward. He welcomed me with a big smile and told me they already had a job for me.

I was surprised, even more so when he explained that the Junior Medical Officer was always in charge of the wardroom's bar.

I hadn't heard before about any traditionally acquired duties. I told Chizy about my three-week experience in Charlottetown, Prince Edward Island, where I had to sign prescriptions so that HMCS Queen Charlottetown's crew could get liquor. I hadn't realized that would be training for this new posting.

It turned out that Chizy did all the work and did it well and cheerfully. All I had to do was to check with him frequently and to buy new liquor supplies when needed. But I did wonder about the origin of this tradition.

Declaring that I needed to know how the bar worked, Chizy set about to teach me. First, I needed to learn was the prices. At fifteen cents, rum and Coke was the most expensive. That was four cents an ounce for the rum and eleven cents for the Coke. Pabst Blue Ribbon beer was three cents for a twelve-ounce bottle. Gin was four cents an ounce, Seagram's VO was five, and blended Scotch whiskey was eight cents.

I was curious as to whether we could actually break even at these prices, but Chizy assured me that we would. We didn't have to pay taxes, so a twenty-four-ounce bottle of gin was only ninety cents. Selling it at four cents an ounce netted us six cents profit. However, due to the allowances for corkage and spillage, there was always more than just twenty-four ounces in the bottle. The profits added up and there was always more than enough.

There were monthly limits on how much each person could spend. Sub-lieutenants were allowed eight dollars a month; a lieutenant like me was allowed twelve, lieutenant-commanders were allowed fifteen, and commanders and above were allowed twenty. Chizy and I would have to check the totals each month and add them to the mess bills.

I was glad Chizy was around to look after it all. It seemed to me that with him in charge, my supervisory job wouldn't be too arduous.

Chapter Three

British Talk First, then Canadian

Eventually, an officer came along to have lunch, introducing himself as Gus Airey, the flight deck engineer.

When I asked what a flight deck engineer did, he explained that he was the guy in charge of the aircraft catapult machinery. He suggested that we have lunch, and then he would show me around the flight deck to help get me oriented.

Lunch finished, we climbed the ladder up one deck to what he said was the hangar deck. It seemed to be filled with airplanes. We went up a nearby ladder to a deck space filled with airplanes. This, Gus explained to me, was the hangar where the planes were serviced and repaired, like an automotive garage. Once we got going, it would be a busy place round the clock. Walking across the hangar deck, I noticed that the steel plates of the hangar deck were welded. Having previously read that this was a new and untested method used on these quickly built ships, I asked him why they weren't riveted.

Gus explained to me that it was unusual and some could think it was a negative, but he didn't agree. With any lateral stress, the rivets could fly off, while if the welding was well-done, that wouldn't happen. All the plates throughout the ship were welded.

We walked across to the starboard side and climbed an enclosed stairway to the flight deck where I would spend most of my time. I would need to know it in detail. When we got up there, I saw that there were two elevators, one fore and one aft, which took the aircraft to and from the flight deck and the hangar. The British called them lifts, but, Gus informed me, we Canadians called them elevators. That caused an unusual announcement when one of the elevators is about to be used; after the bos'n's whistle, the call would be, "Power on the forward (or aft) lift; elevator operators close up." So it was British talk first, then Canadian.

There were small, gun-carrying platforms projecting from the sides that were called sponsons. They were joined together by grilled catwalks. It was the same on the other side of the flight deck. Each sponson had a twenty-millimeter Oerlikon machine gun with a Mark 14 automatic tracking gun sights, an American invention. It was a good one, because it took aiming away from the old 'By guess and by God' method. Some sponsons had high altitude anti-aircraft forty-millimeter Bofors guns. On the stern, there were two artillery guns that fired five-inch shells.

As we walked forward a little, Gus pointed out something I really wanted to see. Off the catwalk was a small medical emergency room.

It was a small cabin about seven feet by twelve; in the centre there was a metal table. Around the periphery was a continuous metal shelf, above which were cabinets. I looked in a few and, yes, they contained medical supplies of one type or another. It would all need to be organized.

We returned to the catwalk, and in a short distance, we entered a much larger room, arranged as a lecture room. Here, the chairs were leather-covered and looked very comfortable. The bulkheads at the front were covered with blackboards, while hanging from the overhead pipes were a large number of model airplanes. I assumed these were for practicing aircraft identification.

This was the aircrew's Ready Room, where they would wait before they went to man their aircraft, to get their briefings, and to hear various lectures. They spent much of their time at sea just waiting. If it was nighttime, it would not be as brightly lit as it was then, but would have dim red lights so that the aircrew could directly go out onto a dark flight deck without having to spend time adapting to the lack of light.

I looked at the room in awe. At that time, I looked up to aircrew as very special people who could fly airplanes and land them on moving ships. This room was their space. It took me some weeks before I could comfortably enter that room and feel really comfortable.

When we got back on the flight deck, Gus pointed to a superstructure that was on the starboard side of the ship and was about two thirds of the way to the bow. He told me that it was called the Island and that it housed the chart room, the wheel house, the bridge, a combat action room, some radar units, and a number of aerials. It was positioned on the extreme starboard side, overhanging the side of the ship, but completely free of the deck. Arrestor wires were positioned about every ten yards, spanning the aft two thirds of the deck. Just before a plane was to land they would be lifted twelve inches or more. The pilot would extend a hook from the tail of his plane that was supposed to pick up one of these wires. The nearer the stern of the ship the plane would land the better, because each wire going forward had increasing tension and pulled the plane to a quicker and quicker stop. If his hook did not pick up any of the wires, wires near the Island would be lifted to form a vertical wire barrier, preventing the plane's further forward progress. The space on which the planes had to land with the ship moving was about three hundred and fifty feet long and seventy feet wide. That was indeed precision flying.

From there, we went up near the bow to see where they did the catapulting.

We walked over to the port side and forward to where there was a longitudinal track in the wooden deck. Gus explained that was where they positioned the aircraft when it was going to be catapulted. The apparatus to do it was down below and it was his job to see that it worked.

To me, it seemed like Gus really got a kick out of doing it.

The longer I was with him, the more I liked him. Of medium height, he was very straightforward, spoke directly, and had enthusiasm, entirely the sort of person on whom I felt I could depend. I'd learned the flight deck was going to be important to me, but at that time I didn't know I would be there for every landing and take-off, nor that I would be the first medical responder at any crash.

I thought this introduction to the flight deck was very helpful and thanked him profusely. It was great to get to know him. I thought he was very special.

When I got back to my cabin, I found my cabin mate had arrived, Lieutenant Alex MacKay, a very friendly, outgoing, and handsome man. He turned out to be an ideal person with whom to live in such quarters.

I soon learned he was an experienced teacher. When I asked him what he was going to do on the ship, he told me he was going to be a schoolmaster for sailors who wanted to advance in rank. He was also going to be a cipher officer.

I was sorry about the lower berth, but he was fine with it as he preferred the top, having been a gymnast in college. He proved this to me by climbing up to his berth, adeptly reaching an overhead pipe, and swinging back down to the deck. He was looking forward to starting each day that way.

It turned out he had another idiosyncrasy; every morning he spent what seemed to me an inordinate amount of time massaging his scalp and brushing his hair. He did have a fine growth of naturally dark wavy hair and insisted such care would help him keep it for a long time. Every morning he warned me, who simply took comb and brush to my hair briefly, that I would soon be bald. A tall well-built young man, he was energetic and soon became very popular with everyone, as well as highly respected for the way he carried out his duties. We would come to call him Schoolie.

A little while later, I saw a naval officer who had two red stripes amongst three gold ones on his sleeves. I knew that he had to be the most important person on the ship as far as I was concerned. I introduced myself and learned he was Lieutenant Commander Walter G. Rice, the Senior Medical Officer. I looked him over very carefully. I noted his eyes were deep set and when he looked at me his upper eyelids were barely visible. To me, that meant he was the sort of person who thought before he made decisions, and the laugh lines at the corner of his eyes indicated a good sense of humor. Modest lines around mouth and firm lips suggested he was not overly talkative. This made me feel that he wasn't the type who would pull rank on me or treat me as a doctor newly out of medical school, even though I was. Immediately I felt sure he was the sort of person with whom we would be able to talk things out if we had any disagreement. Although he was only about five years older than I, he gave me the impression that he had become wise in the ways of the Navy and experienced in other ways beyond his years. In navy terms, I thought he was 'salty' and was sure he would be there, if and when I needed him.

After a few minutes of small talk, he suggested that we go look at the medical facilities. We walked forward on the port side companionway until we came to what was obviously the Sick Bay or Outpatient Clinic. All of our sick berth attendants, commonly known as tiffies, were there and we introduced ourselves to Chief Petty Officer (PO) Hines, a fellow Nova Scotian. He introduced his staff, the tiffies. Walter spoke to them briefly, and said a little about the two of us. Then PO Hines led us forward to our ward where, in addition to an appropriately positioned attendant's station, six individual bunk beds were arranged around the periphery; in the center stood a modern adjustable white hospital bed. That I didn't expect, but it made me feel like it was really a place to look after sick people and where the standards would be high. I was even more impressed when we went into the nearby operating suite, with its overhead operating lights that were married to the operating table. "Just like a real hospital," I heard Carter, one of the tiffies, comment.

But then, both Walter and I noticed the large number of unopened cardboard boxes that were stacked up around the periphery of the room. Hines explained that they were surgical instruments which the staff felt should be unpacked and sorted by the doctors themselves.

Both Walter and I were very pleased with the way all our medical spaces were folded together in a very compact and efficiently arranged unit. Obviously, we had a lot to do, such as making sure the tiffies were well trained. Unpacking and sorting those surgical instruments was going to take both time and thought, as neither Walter nor I having had in-depth training in surgery.

Afterwards, he and I went back to the wardroom and had a long talk over several beers. I told him about me, and I was surprised that he was already partially filled in. He told me he'd been born in Nigeria in 1912, where his parents were Baptist missionaries. In 1938, he received his MD from the University of Toronto and, planning to be a pathologist, had begun a Fellowship in Pathology. Then the war broke out and Walter had felt it was his duty to join up, so in 1940 he'd joined the Canadian Navy and started out examining recruits. The word about was, true or not, that anyone of the physicians who allowed an unfit recruit to get to Halifax would be liable for the recruit's travel expenses home, so they referred all questionable volunteers to the Army or Air Force.

I thought it was what I would have done, too.

He went on to say that at that time the Canadian Navy was so small that it didn't have much need for doctors, so his group of early recruits agreed to be seconded to the Royal Navy. After crossing the Atlantic, they were assigned to Portsmouth and the HMS Victory for an immediate course in naval tradition that included some of the stuff the Royal Navy considered really important. For example, they learned that Nelson did not have heat in his cabin before ten in the morning and, no, it was not proper for Naval Officers to whistle. It was interesting, Walter told me, but a complete waste of time! Of course, in those years, sporadic air raids and duty in the shelters often interrupted their courses.

After that, he'd served on HMS Bradford, one of the fifty former U.S. four stacker destroyers with flush decks. Those destroyers were totally unsuited to the heavy seas of the North Atlantic. They were the group of destroyers that was given to Britain in exchange for a naval base in Trinidad and in Argentia, Newfoundland. 'An absolute necessity', the newspapers had proclaimed.

Personally, I thought it was nonsense. These words were but the publicity tokens for the British giving the bases to the Americans. Both the U.S. Navy and the Royal Navy surely must have known these destroyers would be of no use in the Atlantic.

"They were a disaster, weren't they?" I asked Walter. "I've heard they sometimes rolled as much as fifty degrees."

Yes, he'd been on the Bradford when he figured they had rolled more than that. One time, he'd been sure they were going to capsize.

Walter's luck changed in March of 1941. He was the only Canadian in the first group of twelve medical officers who were selected for a course in aviation medicine at the major naval air bases of Lee-on Solent near Portsmouth and at Yeovilton in southwest England. Naval aviation was still a new concept in the Royal Navy and naval aviation medicine was equally revolutionary in the medical branch. This first ever course put on by the Royal Navy included G-forces, oxygen, high altitude flying, and stress. Then, for two weeks, they'd studied tropical medicine in London. That was conducted at the time of the first one thousand plane raid by the German Luftwasse. Walter told me it was an event to remember. He was lucky to have survived it.

They'd easily recognized that many traditional Royal Navy officers had great difficulty accepting the new reality, such as radar or that surface ships were vulnerable to air attack.

As we sipped our beer, Walter continued to tell his story. He'd had a great time at both of these courses, but his real luck had come when he was one of the two graduates who were sent to Egypt. The others had been assigned to Singapore and Ceylon (Sri Lanka); Walter did not think any of them had survived.

I wanted to know more about what it was like in Egypt.

By April of 1942, all the carriers had been withdrawn from the Mediterranean because of their vulnerability to torpedo and bombing attacks, so their squadrons were detached and based in the desert. Walter had been ordered to join Fleet Air Arm Squadron 805 that was flying Wildcats (F4F's). The sand and flies and tent life had made life miserable, but the squadron had always enjoyed high morale, largely due to the squadron leader, Lieutenant Commander Tim Coode's (DSO) leadership and style. Coode was the hero of the Swordfish attack that back in 1941 torpedoed the Bismarck, after which she could only go in circles. She'd been immediately destroyed.

I was curious as to whether Walter had met any Canadian RCNVR pilots while he was in the desert. I'd heard that there weren't enough Canadians in the Fleet Air Arm to form a Canadian squadron and that was why they had to have a Royal Navy squadron on Nabob.

That was not the real reason. Walter explained that it was because the Canadian navy had always been so focused on corvettes and frigates; no one stopped to think how a naval air force would fit into protecting convoys. It had only been in the past year that they had recognized how effective U-boat hunter groups consisting of an aircraft carrier like Nabob and two destroyers were. He had heard about them and spent two weeks with the United States Navy. When he returned, he began to actively promote adding carriers to the Canadian Navy.

It might have been that the Royal Navy's influence on the Canadian Navy's top brass in Ottawa had slowed its understanding of the role of air power in all kinds of naval warfare. At that time, the Royal Navy had trained all the senior Canadian naval officers and they were very slow to give the Naval Minister the best advice or keep him adequately informed.

When Walter got around to answering the first question, yes, he had known some of the RCNVR pilots when he'd been in the desert. He remembered some as very special people. Of particular note was Hammy Gray from Nelson, British Columbia. Hammy was the only Canadian in the Royal Canadian Navy to win a Victoria Cross. He was one of those rare individuals who had the qualities of absolute fearlessness, leadership, and élan. I think Hammy was a lot like Bobby Bradshaw in our squadron. None of those men Walter told me about had survived.

His voice became husky; he stopped talking and looked away. In a minute or so, he cleared his throat with some beer and then we moved on to a different subject. Walter had been brought home by Ottawa nine months ago. He had just finished a great refresher period as a resident in medicine at the Toronto Western Hospital. Now he was here on Nabob, the one appointment he wanted. In that, he and I were alike.

We concluded that we might have a pretty good time together and that we had a great medical team with our tiffies.

Walter never talked in detail about his experiences, always seeming more interested in telling about the exploits of others. But as time went on, I became more and more aware of what a maturing effect his time in the navy had had. When something went wrong, he always seemed to find part of it that was funny and after a drink or two, his light blue eyes would light up and seem to dance. From the beginning, I felt he was the sort of person I could confide in without reservation and I came to believe he trusted me. It was and remains one of the most satisfying relationships I have ever had. This was a man who was already experienced in fighting Hitler's Nazis.

Chapter Four

Approaching Shallow Waters

All seven days of my days in Norfolk were busy ones as I found my way around the ship, meeting more and more people, especially the aircrew members of Squadron 852. I was surprised to see that all the aircrew wore their wings on the left sleeve of their jacket, just above the cloth rings that denoted their rank. I quite liked it.

One evening I was in a taxi with a few of the aircrew returning from an all-male party in the city, where only beer was served, when it went over a big bump without having slowed down. All of us were tossed up off our seats. Sitting in the back seat, I saw Sub-Lieutenant Don Cash, who was directly in front of me, fly up and hit his head on a cross-bar in the roof of the cab. Almost immediately, a great flow of blood began running down the back of his neck. I managed to stop the bleeding by applying pressure, at the same time attempting to reassure the others by telling them that scalp wounds always bleed furiously and that this was not serious. As soon as we got back to the ship, I sewed up his laceration, my first surgery on the Nabob.

Afterwards I sat down and wrote a long letter to my wife telling her about what had gone on so far, being careful to omit any censorable items, like where we were, where we were going, or sights on shore unique to that community.

During this time in Norfolk I had an experience that truly shocked me; I had my first introduction to the indignities that those American citizens who were called Negroes suffered in the United States. Having been brought up in Nova Scotia where there had never been slavery, our 'coloured' people, as we called them, had full civil rights, although not treated quite as equals, something I never understood. Getting on a bus in downtown Norfolk in which white people like me occupied virtually all the forward seats, I walked to the back where there were quite a number of empty seats and sat down. The first thing I knew, the burly, red-faced driver was standing over me. "You can't sit here." He spoke both loudly and with anger. I recoiled, not knowing what he might do next; he looked that formidable.

I spoke up. "This is a good seat and it's crowded up front."

He insisted that I had to. I didn't see why, as, from the looks on their faces, those *citizens* (I accentuated the word,) sitting near me did not seem to mind. I was not going to move.

And I didn't. Looking around at my fellow travelers, I noted a few what I thought were partially hidden pleased looks.

The driver grudgingly went back to his seat.

I relaxed. I really hadn't known what he might do. I'd had fleeting visions of him picking me up by the scruff of my neck and forcibly moving me forward. But he hadn't. Perhaps my uniform with its Canadian badges on my shoulders protected me.

Another time I noticed that the ferry that went across the harbour had separate entrances, one for Blacks and one for Whites. It was hard for me to believe that here was such discrimination and that it was so evident.

When I got back to the Nabob, I ran into another situation that was also upsetting. In Canadian and British ships there was an old tradition called 'Up Spirits.' At 1100, a representative of each of the sailors' messes, was accompanied by an officer to the rum locker, which in the Nabob was located at the very bottom of the ship near the stern. In addition to the rum, beer, and wine, the various spirits for the officers' Ward Room were also stored there. If an individual did not want his rum ration, he received an extra eight cents a day added to his pay. If he did want it, he received a tot of 150-proof rum (Nelson's Blood) diluted with water. I believe they were supposed to drink it as soon as they received it in mess, but I'm certain that many saved it for a later time. This led to an unfortunate incident that occurred while we were in Norfolk. Apparently, there was a problem of some type in the rum locker. Two dockyard workers were assigned the job of fixing it, which they did. Afterwards they apparently decided that this was a great chance to sample the 150-proof rum that was stored there. They each chose a barrel and lay down on the deck and partially opened their spigot. Drop by drop, the rum fell in their open mouths. Late in the afternoon they had not reappeared. Both were eventually found still in the rum locker, but dead. The diagnosis: acute alcohol intoxication. For whatever reason, legal or other, this episode did not become widely known.

Little by little I learned that this unfortunate episode was not the first that had bedeviled the first three months of the Nabob's life as the first Canadian-manned aircraft carrier. Gus Airey told me that the first occurred on 25 January, 1944; the day the Nabob was to have its Fleet Air Arm squadron land on for the first time. The Nabob, under the command of Captain Horatio Nelson Lay, was steaming at full speed near the mouth of the Fraser River, prepared to accept the aircraft of Squadron 851. Gus told me how everyone had been excited and had crowded the bridge and the flight deck galleries (the goofers) as they waited to see the squadron land on the ship. This was the real deal, a truly historic event. Then he'd heard the navigator warn the captain, "We're approaching shallow waters."

Captain Lay had replied that the charts did not show any; only to have the navigator report that the charts kept changing.

At Lay's insistence, they'd carried on.

The deck landing crew had readied themselves at their stations. The deck landing officer (batsman) held his bats in the ready position. Leading his squadron, Lieutenant Commander Tony Tukes, the commander of Squadron 851, prepared to be the first to land. For this exercise, he had a radio call signal, "X-ray Hickory Charlie." The ship's sign was 'Serious.' Nabob signaled she was ready.

Tony began his approach. Suddenly the ship stopped; the Nabob had run aground.

Captain Lay picked up his radio telephone, "Hello, X-ray Hickory Charlie. This is Serious."

"You're telling me?" Tony responded.

All landing attempts had been cancelled and the squadron had returned, first to Vancouver and then back to Los Alamos, near San Francisco.

The papers in Vancouver took full advantage of the story and on the west coast of Canada, the Nabob became known as the HMS Canada Dry or HMS Sandbob. After many frantic efforts, at high tide on 28 January, a group of tugs from Canada and the United States had pulled her off. Someone raised the question in one of the papers, 'Is Nabob snake-bit?' Certainly she was not off to an ideal start. This was not a good beginning in the fight with Hitler's Nazis. Nor was I happy to learn that we had a captain who ignored advice from his navigator.

A subsequent Court of Enquiry relieved Captain Lay of responsibility for this incident. Although Lay had disregarded the advice of his navigator, he was found not guilty, as it was an uncharted sandbar. This did not make sense to me, as the navigator had told him that it was there.

Gus told me that because Nabob continued to be a Royal Navy ship, manned by Canadians with a Royal Navy Fleet Air Arm squadron, rather than being a Royal Canadian Navy ship, the rations for the crew were the same as on all other Royal Navy ships and did not compare favorably with those on Canadian ships. Furthermore, the Canadians had a higher pay scale than the British, who might be doing a comparable job. Both the Canadians and the British were unhappy. Despite the captain's vigorous representations to both the Admiralty in Great Britain and the naval authorities in Ottawa to correct these deficiencies before the Nabob left Vancouver, these requests were not just denied, they were ignored. Although these discrepancies were obviously going to cause trouble, Captain Lay took the Nabob to sea. That was an obvious mistake.

Gus went on to explain that the trouble didn't take long to come to a head. In mid-February, 1944, when they had a three-day stop in San Diego, the HMS Nabob (being a Royal Navy ship, even though it was Canadian manned) had to follow Home Station scales, an Admiralty rule that restricted the quantity and variety of rations. The Canadians in our crew were not blind. They walked through the US navy supply store and saw the fresh oranges and bananas and knew they were freely available, but not to them. Furthermore, they complained that the size of the Royal Navy rations they were being served was totally inadequate. These were children's portions, they said, and were infuriated.

Added to their unhappiness were some glaring omissions in the accommodations on the ship. There were no proper wash basins, the arrangements in the heads were poor, and the ventilation was inadequate. To make matters worse, NAAFI (the British Navy, Army,

Air Force Institute), which was in charge of canteens on British ships, did not stock items Canadians liked, such as ice cream or Coke syrup. The Nabob was not a happy ship. Morale dropped seriously. Nearing Norfolk, there was talk of a grand scale desertion. Thirty-three men did jump ship upon arrival in Norfolk.

The general unhappiness may have been in part responsible for the actions of some members of the crew as the Nabob passed through the Panama Canal on its way from the Pacific to the Atlantic Oceans. They had a few hours shore leave in Colon, where the combined attractions of cheap rum and very available women overwhelmed these young men. Rounded up by the U.S. and Canadian shore patrols later in the evening, many were too drunk to walk on board and had to be lifted in cargo nets and laid out on the flight deck to sober up, much like the scene portrayed later in the book/movie "Mr. Roberts," in which it was very funny. While there were a number of cases of gonorrhea; fortunately, no one acquired syphilis.

Gus told me about the trip from the Canal as the Nabob headed north to Norfolk, Virginia. Because of the known presence of German submarines in this area, the frigate HMCS New Waterford accompanied the Nabob up the Atlantic coast and the squadron regularly mounted anti-submarine search patrols

Sub-Lieutenant Don Cash later told me about the anti-submarine search he did. He'd taken off in the dark on one such patrol, with his navigator C. D. Wheeler and tail gunner Bernard Blisset. As they'd neared the end of the three-hour scheduled flight, they found that the radio was not working, so they were no longer able to contact the Nabob. It was not unusual for the radio to fail. They re-checked the navigation and started a square search. Cash began watching the fuel gauge with increasing intensity. They began a series of expanded square searches, but they could not find the ship. It could have been because they were not where they thought they were, or the ship was not where it was supposed to be. In any event, Cash finally realized that they were lost. Knowing that Cuba was the nearest land and that his fuel was getting low, he decided to head for where he thought land might be. Suddenly they were over breakers; the whiteness showing up in the dark. They discussed whether to risk a beach landing or a water landing near the shore. Finally, they decided to go off-shore to drop their depth charges, unarmed, and headed to shore. In hopes of seeing the state of the beach, Cash fired his Very pistol. To their amazement, dead ahead of them, runway lights lit up like a gift from the Heavens. With their fuel gauge indicating fumes only, this was it. There would be no going around again. Cash set their Avenger, 'F' for Freddie, down on the runway. Never had he heard a sweeter sound than when their tires kissed that runway. He had no more than turned onto a taxiway when the engine quit, finally out of gas.

They waited there to find out what kind of a reception was going to arrive. Then came a jeep and out stepped an American sailor, fully armed. They immediately realized that they were at the American base in Guantanamo Bay, Cuba.

Cash and his crew had been welcomed warmly and shown a great time. The next morning, they flew back to the Nabob with two American Air Force Hellcats escorting them, because they still didn't have a radio or any other navigational guides. The Americans had notified the Nabob of their survival, but not in time to prevent signals sent to their parents that they were missing. Needless to say, their parents were greatly relieved when they were informed that they had been found.

Immediately, upon the Nabob's arrival in Norfolk, Captain Lay flew to Ottawa. When he returned, there was a rumor, later confirmed, that he'd told the 'naval authorities,' meaning the Admiralty and the Canadians, both of whom had previously ignored his requests, that he would not take the Nabob to sea again until the pay and other inequities were corrected. This time he was successful, as he should have insisted on before he ever took the Nabob out of Vancouver. Now the Canadians would pay for everyone to have Canadian rations and the British were to have their pay elevated to equivalent Canadian scale at Canada's expense. The problems in the heads were corrected while at Norfolk, but some of the irritating problems with NAAFI, apparently a totally impervious and independent organization, lingered on.

What Captain Lay had done impressed me, but I wondered why he hadn't done this before they left Vancouver. His other failure was that his efforts to have the Nabob become a Canadian ship were unsuccessful. However, that was because of the adamant refusal of his uncle,

Prime Minister MacKenzie King, who said that "we pay for all our war equipment we get from the United States; we do not get involved with Lend Lease." In this respect, I agreed with his uncle. But as a result, the Nabob remained a Royal Navy ship and so the Royal Navy Admiralty, not the Canadian Navy, controlled the Nabob's (our) future. I didn't realize at the time how important that would turn out to be. Under Canadian control, we might well have gone to the Atlantic, rather than to the Arctic Ocean, where we became a unit of the British Home Fleet. For the British, it was really a good deal, because they essentially added one carrier, and eventually a second one, without costing them a damn cent.

Chapter Five

Bobby Bradshaw Held No Such Fear

War begets heroes and legends, those men whose names are said in awed whispers as their fellow soldiers speak in wonder about their seemingly superhuman feats. On board the HMS Nabob, we had one such man, Lieutenant Commander R. E. (Bobby) Bradshaw (DSC - 2 Bars), the commanding officer of Squadron 852. He was a legend in the Fleet Air Arm, and everyone seemed to have a story or two to tell.

Bobby belonged to a longtime navy family. His grandfather was a well-known admiral and his father had reached the status of captain before he developed tuberculosis and died. After beginning his education at Sherborne House, Bobby went to Pangbourne Naval Academy. There, from all accounts, he was an excellent student, very popular and a star athlete in every sport. Everything in his upbringing indicated he would be a great leader.

He joined the Navy as an ensign in 1938 and transferred to the Fleet Air Arm in 1939. In October 1940, he was posted as a Midshipman to Albacore Squadron 826 on Formidable, a new carrier. It didn't take long for him to be noticed. Just three months later, the January London Gazette reported that now Sub-Lieutenant Bradshaw was mentioned in dispatches for 'outstanding patience, zeal, cheerfulness and whole-hearted devotion to duty,'

Then in March of 1941, consequent to his participation in the Battle of Marsapan in which the remnant of the Italian Navy was essentially destroyed, he was awarded another mention, 'for bravery and enterprise'. A third 'Mention in Dispatches' followed in April and followed almost immediately by the award of a Distinguished Service Cross, which was awarded "For sustained courage, skill and enterprise in many air operations by night and day against the enemy during months of duty in air operations."

Of course, I'd seen him at a distance in the wardroom, but he was always talking to someone and I didn't want to interrupt. But before long, I happened to be sitting beside him at lunch. I found him to be a very friendly, handsome young man of average height, who you'd never know was already such a hero. From the way he moved, I thought he undoubtedly was a very good athlete. He wasn't wearing a normal naval uniform, but a rather worn army khaki army battle jacket that had only one epaulet. Nowhere to be seen were the two DSCs (Distinguished Service Cross) I'd been told he'd been awarded. As a matter of fact, the one time I ever saw them when he was not on parade, was once when I was chatting with him in his cabin. It was in the evening and he was already in his pajamas. It was then that I saw both of them, sewn to the seat of his pajamas. He had none of the aloofness or formality about him that I'd heard characterized many squadron leaders, many of whom seemed to be very much involved with having achieved such a status.

One time, when I was about to leave his cabin, he surprised me by offering me a pair of fleece-lined flying boots he had used when flying open cabin Albacores, but now had absolutely no use for. He felt that since I lived in a cold country, I may have use for them, as they were in his way. I was happy to accept them for I was sure they would be just great to wear on a cold winter's day at home. But this showed me how generous he was. It somehow fit in with my having observed that he and all the members of his squadron, not just the aircrew, were on a first name basis during leisure hours. This was most unusual, especially in the Royal Navy. I thought it was probably a good thing for him that he was on a Canadian ship, where rank held little sway and informality was the way things were. There was nothing about him in the way he looked or acted that would make me think he had done the extraordinary feats I'd heard he'd performed. I wondered how anybody who apparently had done so much could be so laid back.

One of the pilots, Eric Roberts, told me a story that explained why the squadron held Bobby in such high regard.

After forming up in Quantum, Massachusetts, the squadron had conducted many exercises that led them to stay overnight in Lewiston, Maine. Naturally, they formed friendships there. At Christmas, Bobby said everybody would have three days' leave; half the crew's leave would be before Christmas and half would be after. He wanted everyone to use this time as a navigation exercise (a Navex); each crew choosing where they wanted to go. Roberts's crew had developed friends in Lewiston, Maine, so they flew up there and spent those three days with them, apparently having a wonderful time. The whole squadron felt that Bobby had bent the rules to give them the holiday of their choice.

That conversation led me to wonder about how Bobby had spent his Christmas, so when I ran into him, I asked him. He told me about how their Senior Naval Officer at Squantum had invited him and Tony Tukes to spend a few days with a friend of his in Providence, Rhode Island. They'd always called him 'Steady,' and Bobby had been delighted to see him again. They'd served together in 826 Squadron in the desert. Tukes was now the CO of Squadron 851 which just preceded them at Squantum. However, in Providence, he'd embarrassed Bobby when he'd introduced him to the guests at the party; he told them that he was the most decorated pilot in the Fleet Air Arm and then, if that wasn't enough, he went on to say that Bobby was the only chap to have joined a squadron as a midshipman and subsequently become its Commanding Officer (CO). And he'd emphasized that Bobby had done it all while in the desert.

I told him about my Christmas on Prince Edward Island with my wife. His only comment was, "I wish I'd been with you."

Everyone was on a first-name basis and they all seemed so comfortable with one another and with Bobby.

Although I did not have the same experience with the Navy, I also found it unusual. I'd been with this squadron for only a short time, but from talking to them, I knew that to a man, they would follow him wherever he'd lead them. I believed him to be an extraordinary leader.

Walter, who had spent time in the desert during this war, had also heard stories about Bobby. Everyone in the desert had known about Bobby; his attitude, his courage, and the support he gave to others in his squadron who were less talented. But Walter had never met him until boarding the Nabob, as he'd been with a Wildcat (F4F) fighter squadron and Bobby was a member of an Albacore Squadron, 826. They would not have had contact. But Walter had indeed heard some stories.

Albacores were very solid aircraft, but not the swiftest ever developed. Before and during the time General Rommel (the Desert

Fox) drove the British out of Libya and all the way to El Alamein near Cairo in Egypt, Squadron 826 flew night sorties against the German forces. Their planes would take off from one desert landing field and, later that night, land for the night on another field farther east. According to a member of his squadron, Bobby, after making two sorties, routinely had had his aircraft refueled and his stock of flares and bombs renewed so he could take off to make a third attack. Not even his Commanding Officer had known about these extra flights.

Apparently, Walter told me, these night bombing attacks had been much to Bobby's liking. Not only had he acted as a 'pathfinder' for the RAF bombers, but apparently, he would drop his flares to light up the target and then dive down to bomb the bombing point, reportedly very accurately. Then he'd continue down to low altitudes and strafe any of the enemy he could find. His observer said one time that Bobby could make his Albacore do anything he wanted it to do and that he should have been a fighter pilot.

My personal feeling was that Bobby had acted as if he wanted to kill as many Nazis as he could, though he never said as much. Even though it went contrary to my oath of healing as a physician, I confess to having felt the same way. The philosophy of Nazism, the idea that one particular race and creed was entitled to rule all others, and that persons of other races, creeds, abilities, and natures were less human and ought to be subjugated, occupied, imprisoned, enslaved, or eliminated, was abhorrent to me. We had to get rid of those who espoused these dangerous ideals, or they'd change our world completely. I found it remarkable that Bobby never showed that attitude in speech, though his actions in the skies said otherwise.

Walter made no comment, just went on as if I hadn't said a word. Then after a minute or so, he explained how in June of 1942, when the British forces finally stopped the Germans at El Alamein, there were those in the squadrons who were afraid that even that line wouldn't hold. Bobby held no such fear. He'd told everyone that this is the field, Dekheila, where all would continue to operate from, and where, when one was not on flying duty, he would continue to enjoy the beds as well as the pleasures of Alexandria and Cairo.

I wanted to hear more stories, so Walter kept going.

During the time when the British forces were being built up, Bobby had a week's leave and visited a friend in a Royal Air Force fighter squadron. They were flying Hurricanes (fighter planes which flew with Spitfires in the Battle of Britain in 1941). Bobby had always wanted to fly one of them, but had never been checked out on one. But when he saw a Hurricane actually sitting right in front of him on the tarmac, the temptation was overwhelming. He persuaded his friend to check him out, so he'd be able to fly it. Then both he and his friend each got in their planes and took off for a little flight. Soon they were over enemy territory and met a German airplane. They both attacked, but it was Bobby who shot it down. Because he wasn't supposed to be there, he reported it was his companion, not he, who had done it and then quickly left for Alexandria.

During the hurried retreat from Libya in the spring of 1942, one of the squadron's Albacores was left behind on their abandoned airfield. When Bobby heard about this the next morning, he talked one of the other pilots in the squadron into flying him back to the abandoned field, now occupied by the Germans. They landed. Bobby got out of the plane, walked across to the abandoned Albacore, as the Germans watched, got in, started the engine and flew it back to the squadron.

After Rommel's defeat in the second Battle of El Alamein, Squadron 826 pursued the retreating German forces, bombing them at every opportunity, day after day, all the way to Tripoli. There, that September, Bobby was awarded a Bar to his DSC, 'for bravery and devotion to duty in air operations in the Western Desert.'

In early 1943, Bobby was promoted to Lieutenant Commander and given command of his squadron. Interestingly, this was the first time ever that a person who had joined the same squadron as a midshipman (not an officer) had become its commander. At that time, altogether Bobby had amassed an incredible 1,457 hours of operational service (470 at night); nearly all in Albacores. Finally, after the invasion of Sicily, he was given an extended leave, after two and a half years (1340 flying hours) of continuously flying against the enemy. From there, he was posted to the United States to become the commander of a new squadron, Squadron 852.

Walter finished with telling me that the one thing about Bobby that everyone agreed was that he was absolutely fearless.

I was amazed by all the stories. I wondered if there might there be even more. Well, I didn't know how Bobby got his first Distinguished Service Cross. So later that afternoon, I came across some of the aircrew standing on the flight deck. One of them invited me to join them watching three new Avengers being brought on board. I wondered why so many aircraft needed to be replaced.

Parky (Lieutenant Ralph Parkinson), Bobby's observer, told me the story in his broad Lancashire accent that I still had trouble understanding. When they'd left San Francisco about the middle of February, the USS Ballard, a destroyer, and Blimp K-115 had accompanied them. The very next day, they'd begun flying operations. The very first pilot to take off was Lefty Batten, who alone in his Avenger, lost power immediately and went into the sea, dead ahead of the ship. The plane was lost; but fortunately, the officer of the watch, Lieutenant Jackson Fraser, was alert and managed to order a change in the course sufficient that the ship did not run over the aircraft. The blimp swooped down and dropped an inflated life raft close to the starboard wing. Batten climbed out of his cockpit, walked out on the wing and got into the raft. He'd been lucky; didn't even get his feet wet. Before long, a motor whaleboat from Ballard picked him and brought him back to the Nabob. The crews had discovered that the Avenger floated for two minutes before sinking, which was useful information. They'd also been pleased with the American response.

A second aircraft was so badly damaged it had to be written off when Keith Stevens landed without a tail hook and hit the barrier at high speed and nosed up on the deck. Keith was also the pilot a few days later, when the batsman gave him a wave-off, signaling him not to land, because he was too high. But he was only five feet above the deck and as he accelerated to go around again, his tail-hook caught in the top wire of the barrier. This swung his aircraft around and down, so that it hit and destroyed an aircraft parked in front of the barrier, as well as damaging his own starboard wheel. No one was hurt in any of these events, but all these three aircraft had to be replaced.

I was rather amazed that there were no injuries, but Bill Reeks pointed out to me that none of them were like crashes on land. The forward speed of these aircraft was only thirty or forty knots faster than the ship was going, so they weren't high-speed crashes. And Grumman had designed these planes to take a lot of punishment.

All of the squadron members seemed to be quite glad to have been taken on by Bobby into the 852 Squadron and happy to have him there.

With that, we all went off to the wardroom. The beer was on me.

Chapter Six

On the Starboard Catwalk

Probably stimulated by knowing that this next day, 18 March, we were going to leave our berth in Norfolk and sail up the coast to New York, I was awake even before the daily piercing trill of the bos'n whistle and his morning words came over the intercom, "Wakey, Wakey, Wakey, Rise and Shine, etc." After breakfast, I was up on the flight deck, all eyes and ears to find out when and what was going on. I had already chosen a place to stand—on the starboard catwalk near the first arrestor wire. In this position, my head was well above the level of the flight deck and I could see any aircraft approaching the stern. At the same time, I could see a New Zealander, Lieutenant Gavin Waite, RNZVR, the Deck Landing Controller (commonly called the batsman) manipulate his bats (at night, his electrified wands) as he directed the pilots who came in to land on the Nabob. If I were looking forward, this same position allowed me to see the full length of the flight deck. This is where I stood for every landing or take-off that occurred during the entire time I was on the Nabob.

The weather was perfect for flying; clear sunny sky and a fifteen-knot wind. This favorable weather provided many opportunities to observe Gavin's antics. His position was directly opposite me on a platform on the port side of the ship. Standing there with his bats, he directed every aircraft to a landing on the flight deck. Ordinarily, a group of planes intending to land would circle the ship in single file, fly along the starboard side towards the bow, make a left turn in front of the ship, fly aft along the port side until past the ship and make another left turn and form a line, behind the flight deck. As soon as a pilot brought his plane in line with the ship, his eyes focused on the batsman, who now was in charge of the aircraft. If the plane was coming in too low, Gavin raised his arms, making a vee; if it was coming in too high, his arms were down and away from his body. Gavin ordered changes of speed by bringing his arms nearer or farther away from his body. To abort the landing and go round again, he made a circular motion with his entire arm. To tell the pilot it was time to cut the engine and let the aircraft drop onto the deck, he drew his arm and bat horizontally across his neck. There were other maneuvers that he used too, but I never found out the meanings of all of them.

As I arrived on deck, a group of strapping young men, the flight deck crew, wearing overalls and blue skull caps that were strapped under their chins, were pushing the first of three Avengers, each with an identifying letter (P, Q, or R) painted on the fuselage, off the aft elevator as if the plane was a toy. P was Watson's, Q, Davis's and R, Steven's; all were New Zealand pilots. The flight deck crew ranged the three aircraft near the stern, with Watson's aircraft being slightly ahead of the other two, all with their wings still folded. The aircrews, pilots, observers (navigator) and tail-gunners all climbed on board, and in a short time all the pilots started their engines to warm them up and began to run through their pre-flight check lists. On a signal from the Commander-Flying on the bridge, Watson, in the foremost plane, moved his plane forward to a broad white line that ran intermittently down the middle of the deck. When he was well clear of the propellers of the other two, he unfolded his wings and ran the engine up to full throttle, his brakes hard on. When all was ready, he released the brakes, the chocks holding the wheels were pulled away and he began his take off. With the Nabob heading into the wind at fifteen knots and a natural wind of seventeen knots, there was an initial forward speed of thirty-two. By the time the plane ran out of deck space, it had added thirty-two knots, giving a total air speed of sixty-four knots per hour. That they could become airborne at that speed amazed me. I noticed that after lift-off, some pilots nosed their aircraft slightly down toward the water to gain air speed. Others put the nose up a little, which always made me worry they would stall, but they never did. Both methods seemed to work.

It didn't take me long to recognize that the pilots had idiosyncrasies. Bill Black, a six footer from the Isle of Mann, had a landing approach that was unique. He always started from much farther behind the ship than any of the others and came straight in, steadily losing altitude and virtually never needing any adjustments from Gavin. On the other hand, Keith Stevens, a short New Zealander had to, even with a cushion, peer out his side window to see the batsman. This meant that soon after he completed the port side run, he had to make a tight left turn, straightening out just before he came over the round arm of the flight deck. Bobby Bradshaw, the squadron leader, seemed to pay no attention to Gavin. Of course, when he began landing on flight decks as mid-shipman in the thirties, there weren't any batsmen and he continued to act as if they still didn't exist. However, even though some of his landings were a bit hairy, he always landed successfully. Others had the ability to sense whether their approach was right and needed a little help from Gavin.

The squadron had not flown since the Nabob arrived in Norfolk, and they were delighted to be in the air again, and they flew that way. One way they showed how they felt was by doing a number of maneuvers after they returned from their anti-sub patrol, such as flying low over our deck, low enough that I dove flat on my stomach (I never got used to that) as the planes sped by. They called it 'beating up the ship,' and I enjoyed their high spirits. But at the end of the day, there were two pilots about whom I was concerned. One was Sub-Lieutenant Lord, who showed that he could get his plane to do anything he wanted it to do, but who I felt seemed to fly very close to his edge of safety. If he made one little mistake, there could be a disaster. Perhaps he was a fighter pilot by temperament. The other pilot I began to worry about was Sub-Lieutenant Batten, who I considered to be a very iffy pilot. However, I recognized that this was the first time I'd seen them fly and my opinion was not worth much. I kept my thoughts to myself.

My plate was certainly full after that first day of watching all that activity on the flight deck. My only problem was that the darkness came too early; the day too short. I went to bed that night thinking how lucky I was to be on the Nabob.

Chapter Seven

Luxuriously Comfortable to the End

The next morning, 19 March, we were tied up at the docks in Staten Island. At breakfast, we heard the disappointing news that our planes were to be stored in the hangar deck, and forty-six Mustang fighter planes were going to be fastened to our flight deck. We were to carry them to the United Kingdom, presumably for the United States Air Force. We were to be essentially a freighter. This meant no flying. The squadron had envisaged flying anti-U Boat patrols all the way across the Atlantic, as had I. But it was not to be, and nobody was happy about it. I had the thought that at least that state of affairs would give me more time to get those boxes of instruments unpacked.

Later that morning I was looking through the most recent Naval Report and read an article which noted that the very successful USS Block Island, a sister ship of the Nabob, had been sunk after being hit by three torpedoes off the Canary Islands in late May. What was notable, the article stated, was that out of all the CVEs like Nabob that had been torpedoed, she was the first one that hadn't blown up and the first in which more than ten of her crew survived.

Earlier, I'd been told that we were supposed to sleep with our clothes on, an idea that didn't appeal to me in any way. Now, with this added information, I decided I should take advantage of being in New York to see if I could find some sort of comfortable sleep wear. My thinking was that if I was going to be blown up while in bed, at least I would have been comfortable to the end. I marked a shopping trip as a must-do.

On two different days, I noticed that we were loading a great deal of lumber, not the more commonly-used two-by-four-inch scantling, but six-by-six-inch lumber, a size we called deal in Nova Scotia. Somebody had already told me we had already loaded quite a bit of this lumber in Vancouver and even Norfolk. I didn't see where it was stored and had no idea what it was for, but one of the shipwrights told me that we couldn't have too much of it. The skipper knew what he was doing. To me, it was a mystery. I had no idea why timber belonged on an aircraft carrier.

I don't know how it happened, but the second day we were in Staten Island, Don Cash received an invitation to the Café Rouge in the Hotel Pennsylvania in New York. He organized four or five of us, all the others being aircrew, and we took the ferry to the terminal in Manhattan and, not being familiar with the New York subway, a taxi to the Hotel Pennsylvania. The head waiter of the Rouge Room ushered us to a prominent table. There we were surrounded by well-dressed diners and dancers, who were enjoying not only the food, but also Woody Herman's orchestra that was arranged before us on a slightly elevated stage. I'm sure we all thought it a very elegant scene. Don still had a bandage around his head that resulted from his taxi-caused laceration in Norfolk. Immediately this young, good-looking, apparently wounded aviator attracted attention, and the rest of us were the beneficiaries. Offers of food and any kind of drink one could think of came from all directions. It was almost embarrassing, especially for me, as I had no wings on my sleeve, nor had I done anything to deserve such treatment. Woody Herman's music was great throughout, but one time the band played a medley that included, *I'll Be Seeing You In All the Old Familiar Places, Don't Fence Me In,* and *We'll Meet Again,* "especially dedicated to our brave British airmen," Woody announced. We thoroughly enjoyed the evening and after thanking everyone in sight, we returned to the Nabob feeling no pain.

The next day, I heard that two of our pilots, Angus Watson and Eric Roberts, had gone to Harlem for a wonderful evening listening to the music of Duke Ellington.

Two days before we were scheduled to sail, 23 March, I still had not done my shopping for sleepwear. Late in the afternoon, I hurriedly got myself together and dashed for the ferry to Manhattan. This time I had an opportunity to see and admire the Statue of Liberty, which I knew to be an inspiration for all Americans, but especially American sailors as they came into New York. Having learned by now something of the subway system, I got up to the Abercrombie and Fitch store on

5th Avenue without difficulty. I tried to explain to each sales person that came up to me what my problem was. On our ship, we were supposed to sleep each night in our clothes. I did not find that very attractive and I wanted something simple that I could slip into easily.

One after another, each salesperson said, "You want pajamas." But I tried to explain that I did not want the routine cotton ones that buttoned up in the front.

I finally gave in, but the pajamas I finally had to choose were silk, a very bright orange. If I was going to die by being blown up in the middle of the night, at least I'd be luxuriously comfortable to the end and the colour wouldn't matter. I departed the store with my special night wear in a package that had Abercrombie and Fitch printed in large letters. I hadn't been aware that buying from them also meant that I had to advertise for them.

As I was about to leave the store, one of the men who had been helping me, told me that if I was looking for something to do for the evening, I should go to a United Service Organization (USO).

I thanked him, and, after a quick dinner, I did go to the nearby USO that he suggested. By this time, it was almost eight and most of the interesting things, like theater tickets and Radio City activities were all gone. The only item that looked as if it might be fun was a dance (reception) by Smith College in the Roosevelt Hotel. That was quite close, so I was soon introducing myself to the young woman in charge, a graduate of Smith. There were about fifteen service men there, all younger than I, and all very much focused on the young women with whom they were dancing. The hostess and I danced once, not too successfully, so we spent the rest of the evening just chatting. Finally, almost everyone cleared out, so when she said, "It's pretty late, would you mind showing me home?" I was in no hurry, so I agreed.

When our cab got to Park and 87th street, she said that this was near where she lived. There was a small bar nearby, and we decided to go in to have a drink. After a half hour or so, we were about to leave when I saw a junior paymaster from our ship, who I'd only seen before at a distance. He was obviously very drunk, barely able to stand up. We tried to be very inconspicuous, but he saw us and immediately plunked himself down in our booth. We took this as a signal for me to finish taking my date home and, as we got up, pointedly told him so, hoping that he would stay behind. My date reminded me not to forget my parcel. The young paybob insisted on accompanying us the one or two blocks to her apartment building. During this walk, it became evident he didn't know what city he was in, what his name was, what time it was, what ship he was from, or when we were going to sail. Drunk-sitting duties were certainly not something I wanted to undertake, and I was annoyed. However, he was from our ship and I felt that I had to look after him. I couldn't just abandon him in his condition. Any number of awful things could have happened to him.

I'd noted a subway station near where we'd had drinks, so I steered him in that direction. But when I got there, knowing it was a long ride to the ferry terminal and that it involved at least one transfer, I wasn't sure that it was a good idea to take him on a subway train. What if he passed out or started vomiting or became objectionable to the other riders? So instead of taking him on the subway at 86th Street, we began to walk. Our walk was irregular and spasmodic, as I guided him as best I could, block after block, until finally we reached the 42nd Street subway station. There was nothing about this walk that was fun. By this time, I was tired and he seeming to be somewhat more sober, so I felt I could risk him as a passenger on the subway. After a few subway stops, several seamen from the Nabob came on board. I explained the situation and they willingly took over and guided him through the transfer, onto the ferry and the bus trip back to the ship. Needless to say, I had not found this walk of some forty-odd blocks in the middle of the night in New York particularly enjoyable, so as I got into my bunk, I was still annoyed and very tired, but felt I had done what had to be done. I noted that when I tossed my parcel from Abercrombie and Fitch into a drawer, it was three in the morning.

Chapter Eight

Fog Buoy

By late afternoon the next day, I'd recovered from the previous night's episode and spent much of the afternoon working in the Sick Bay. Our new tiffie had continued to impress everyone with his knowledge and energy; a real winner. When we sailed; however, he was seasick immediately and out of commission.

Later on, I ran into my bunkmate Schoolie, who always seemed to know all that what was going on. He let me in on the latest news. We were going to have fifteen English children and their mothers with us. They were some who have spent the worst of the war years in Canada and were now returning home. "Are you a registered baby-sitter?" he joked.

I'd just been liberated from med school and hospitals, and kids normally had to be sick before I'd look after them. But since Schoolie was used to having healthy kids around all the time in school, I figured he should be nominated.

I'd more or less forgotten about this conversation when I walked into the nearest door to the wardroom for a before dinner drink. Looking around, I saw on the other side of the room a tall, slender, poised, and well-groomed young woman with dark hair and classic facial features. Immediately I recognized her as trophy-level woman, completely surrounded, two deep, by my fellow officers. My immediate reaction was admiration for her beauty. But with all these men around her being higher ranked and undoubtedly more sophisticated than I, I figured there was no way she would even give me a second look. I didn't even pause, just kept on going to the bar. Barely had I gotten there and even before I could give Chizy my order, I found her beside me, her previous admirers left behind on the other side of the room. "Hi," she said," I'm Jo Dewsbury. Are you going to buy me a drink?"

I was astonished. I hadn't known she'd even seen me.

Partially recovering my composure, I managed to say," Sure, what'll it be?"

We had a couple of drinks and sat together for a while until she had to leave to be with her four-year-old daughter at dinner. She told me that her husband, a Royal Navy psychiatrist, was stationed at the Naval Air Base at Lee-on-Solent, near Portsmouth, and that they had a home near there, built in the sixteenth century. Of course, she was looking forward to getting home. She had enjoyed her years in Winnipeg with her daughter, except for its long and very cold winters, but she'd never seen such a social place before; especially at Christmas time. For the whole month, there was a cocktail party somewhere every night, sometimes two, always at somebody's home. The servers were always middle-aged women wearing black dresses with white aprons who used silver trays to offer glasses of Scotch whisky or Canadian rye.

This kind of attention from such a beautiful woman was not something I was used to coping with. Maybe it was, I thought, ego-enhancing, but I couldn't help but thinking that there might be more to the situation than I knew. Perhaps she had noticed my red rings on the sleeves of my uniform, knew I was a doctor, and might have some undisclosed reason for wanting to know me. However, over time, none developed, so it remained a mystery. I supposed that Anne might be jealous, but I hadn't instigated the relationship and didn't anticipate that it would amount to more than a pleasant, innocent friendship as we crossed the Atlantic Ocean. Having an affair never crossed my mind.

We talked quite frequently during this trip across the Atlantic to Liverpool. Having her along to talk to and look at leavened the ten days of the otherwise unremarkable voyage. I enjoyed our walks on the flight deck, all the while dodging the anchored Mustangs. At meal times, she was with her daughter and the other members of the returning English wives and children, none of whom I got to know other than superficially.

The next morning, 23 March, as soon as we were clearly out of the New York Harbour, I found my way to our foremost sponson. I wanted to see our bow spray and whether it was anything like what Joshua

Slocum, a Nova Scotian, the first person to sail around the world alone, had written *in Sailing Around the World* in 1900. As he crossed Massachusetts Bay that day, "every particle of water thrown into the air became a gem, and the Spray, bounding ahead, snatched necklace after necklace from the sea, and as often threw them away." I had been struck by this passage and wondered whether, by chance, our converted freighter might do the same. It didn't. While there certainly was a prow spray, it did not live up to Slocum's poetic description.

This time the Nabob was not alone, but a component of convoy, UT-10. Nineteen of the ships were from New York, the other seven from Boston. Led by a cruiser, the USS Cincinnati, and under the command of a commodore, the ships were arranged in columns, with twelve US destroyers dashing around the periphery of the convoy. It was an important convoy, we were told, because the passenger ships carried many thousand American soldiers destined for what turned out to be the Normandy invasion, while the freighters were loaded to the gunnels with military equipment and supplies.

One night there was a fog that was so heavy that it was impossible to see any of the other ships and, in particular, the ship immediately ahead. To prevent colliding, all the ships streamed a fog-buoy on a long rope from the stern. The phosphorescence was bright enough so that the officer of the watch could focus on it and keep proper station. Lieutenant Jackson Fraser, who had the 0200 watch, was known to be a very conscientious man who took great pride in his seamanship. About 0300, when the fog was at its worst, he noticed that the phosphorescent fog buoy drawing away. He assumed the other ship must have increased its speed. That was odd, he thought, but he ordered what he considered an appropriate increase in the Nabob's speed. A short time later, he noticed that the buoy was again drawing ahead. Again he ordered an increase. The Nabob's original speed was ten knots. His first increase was to twelve knots. Now it was thirteen and still not keeping up with the phosphorescence ahead. Suddenly through the fog, the stern of the ship ahead emerged. Fraser shouted to the helmsman, "Hard a starboard," and signaled the engine room. "Slow speed ahead." Nabob moved sharply to the right, narrowly missing the other ship.

For some reason unknown to us, the ship ahead had been pulling in its fog buoy. From that time on, Lieutenant Fraser had earned himself a nickname, "Fog Buoy (pronounced boy) Fraser."

During the next two consecutive days, we encountered a significant storm. Many of our officers and crew were seasick, and not many showed up for meals. The few unaffected children enjoyed how plates on the long dinner table slid from one end to the other, if not stopped or tied down. The dining room chairs were similarly mobile, but now firmly fixed in place. I continued to eat at all the meals, but had little appetite and felt tired from the increased physical difficulty of walking on ever-changing walkways or even just standing up. At night the ship would roll relatively slowly to port and then back to starboard. In the beginning, when a roll stopped at each extreme, I wondered if it was going to go on farther so that we'd capsize. But after a while, I decided that I couldn't do anything about it and that I might just as well go to sleep.

However, the storm caused modest alterations of our course that took us deeper into the Gulf Stream and closer to the Azores. That meant warmer weather as well as sighting such unusual creatures as several spectacular Portuguese man-of-war, their colourful air-filled bladders resembling an old-time ship under full sail, with strings of stingers, containing poisonous venom, extending thirty to a hundred feet or more.

With the exception of these stormy days, I spent most of my time and energy during our trans-Atlantic voyage in our surgery suite with the tiffies, often with Walter. The ten heavy cardboard boxes, each about four feet tall and three by three feet in horizontal dimensions, were still standing where we had first seen them. Although I'd assumed it would be a dreary task to unpack them and sort out their contents, that's not how it turned out. We all adopted the attitude, "we wonder what treasures we'll find in this box," as we opened each box and examined each item. While neither Walter nor I were trained surgeons, both of us had had a modicum of surgical training and experiences. This meant that either he or I knew the purpose of most of the instruments, although we might not know whether the set of forceps was an Addison or an Allis, or another of the half dozen types of forceps. So it went, one box after another. Some instruments were quite easy to identify, like a mouth gag, or probe, or needle holder (only four different types). But then came the retractors, of which there were at least twenty different types. We had one whole box full of neurosurgical instruments, which we more or less put aside, thinking we were very unlikely to use them. Sometimes we had vigorous discussions about some of them, but it was fun; everyone was involved, especially for Hines and a tiffie named Carter. Little by little we figured out the purpose of virtually every individual instrument and organized them all in what we thought was a reasonable order. By the time we were finished, we felt our surgery suite was ready for use.

Carter knew how to run the autoclave and so was in charge of washing and sterilizing our findings. Hines had been trained as an x-ray technician and demonstrated he knew how to use it. In one way or another, all the tiffies took part in this adventure. Despite our frustrations and our little arguments, I think we all had a good time and had gotten to know each other very well.

During this voyage, most of our more than one hundred officers assembled at the bar before dinner to have a drink, the most popular being Pabst Blue Ribbon beer, of which we consumed about one hundred bottles a day. Some drank rum and coke, others VO whiskey and a few had gin, mostly as a pink gin (a gin with a drop or two of Angostura bitters). Each drink of spirits was but an ounce, and there were limits. Of course, Chizy had the job of recording each drink bought. Only one senior officer, a former merchant mariner, was a regular in the sense that every morning at eleven o'clock, he came to the wardroom and had a "hot milk," a mixture of rum and milk. "My health drink," he said.

Both before and after dinner, we often sang, usually the pop songs of the day, sometimes more ribald tunes, such as the Fleet Air Arm (FAA) favorite, A25. Its first verse of many, went: "*I fly for a living, I fly just for fun, I'm awfully anxious to hack down the Hun, But as for deck landings alone in the dark, As I told* Wings *this morning, fuck that for a start*", together with the chorus, "*Cracking show, I'm alive, I still have to render my A25.*" Another popular tune was the Canadian Navy Volunteer song: "*Roll along Wavy Navy, roll along, Roll along Wavy Navy, roll along, We joined for the money and the fun, The money there is none and the fun has just begun. Roll along Wavy Navy, roll along,*" amongst many other verses. Of course we had a pianist. Don Cash could do it all and well. After dinner, conversation, chess, poker or bridge and reading occupied the time. We all enjoyed ourselves.

One drill I never got used to was Dawn Action Stations. That simply meant getting out of bed when the alarm sounded and going to one's action station and staying there until the All Clear was announced. Getting up at dawn has never been one of my favorite sports, and being awakened by loud gongs did not make the experience more pleasurable. However, we were told that the intense darkness just before dawn was a favorite time for U-Boats to attack, so getting up in the damp cold, which at sea characterized that time of day, seemed to be a rational thing to do. Apparently, the same reasoning held for dusk as well, so we had dusk Action Stations also.

A day or two later we had become in range of enemy aircraft based in France, we were issued steel helmets. I took mine down to my cabin and tucked it away. We didn't have any raids and I don't remember ever seeing anyone wearing one.

On 1 April, Captain Lay gave a short speech in which he explained that we were only seven hundred and fifty miles to go so we would probably be in Liverpool late on Monday night. We were only six hundred miles from the French coast, so now we could have an air attack at any time. At 1300 in the afternoon, all officers and men who had received steel helmets were to to wear them when on the flight deck today. We would not have more than thirty seconds' warning of an attack.

No such attack occurred so there was no need to wear steel helmets.

Because all the aircrew had basic seamanship training before they began their flight training, they had duties as Officer of the Watch during our trans-Atlantic voyage. Pampas Brown, a New Zealand pilot, was an Officer of the Watch the night of 31 March. Just after mid-night, it was dark, other ships in the convoy barely visible, and Pampas was leaning on a bench, not noticing the foot lever that was just ahead of him. He nodded off and as he did, his arm depressed the lever. Suddenly the ship's siren went off. This was a signal that a submarine had penetrated the convoy and for all the ships to immediately disperse, a mistake that was quickly recognized and cancelled. No harm done. Pampas, totally embarrassed, was more than happy when his watch came to an end.

But it was not over. Bobby Bradshaw, seeing this episode as an opportunity to introduce a little fun into what was a rather dull trip, notified Pampas that morning he would be court-martialed that afternoon. In preparation for this, the Wardroom was slightly re-arranged. A chair for the judge and prosecutor, who of course would be Bobby, sat on a dais and a large black sheet was hung from a wire, thus shielding from view anybody to the right side of the chair. About ten minutes before five, I joined the pilots and observers and sat down, totally hidden from where the court was to be held. Promptly on the hour two large seamen, dressed as if they were shore patrol men, escorted Pampas, not a big man, to a place facing the elevated chair, and stood behind him. Bobby then arrived, carrying a scroll, and seated himself in the chair. Partly unrolling the scroll, Bobby read the charge: "That you, Pampas Brown, did at 0057 on the thirty first of March press the tit at the fore end of the Bridge, thereby causing one prolonged blast of the siren for five seconds duration on the siren, causing many frantic calls on the R/T, also losing 0.000072 lbs. of steam pressure which reduced the ship's speed by one and three quarters revs, delaying the ships arrival in U. K. by one minute and thirty two seconds.

"I do hereby adjudge the said M. R. Browne, alias Pampas Joe, to be deprived of seven good conduct badges, stoppage of tomato juice for forty-two days, deprived seven days' passionate leave (first three days on oysters) and every lunch hour to provide a beer for the first officer of the watch, the second officer of the watch and the squadron CO for thirty days.

"Before awarding this punishment, I did, on 31 March, in the presence of the Accused and Lieutenant Parkinson, investigate the matter, and having heard the evidence of Joe Deadlight, Peter Spunyarn, and Lieutenant Commander Rigney, the CO of the Watch and others as well as what the accused had to offer in his defense, I consider the charge to be substantiated against him. Taking into account that this is the 964th offence to be registered against him while serving in 852 Squadron, I judge him to be punished as aforesaid.

Given under my hand on board His Majesty's Ship "Canada Dry" at sea on 31 March, 1944."

Pampas looked pale and sweat had gathered on his forehead. He started to respond, but Bobby looked down on the scroll and intervened. "Oh, now I see here that all charges have been dropped. You are free, Pampas Brown. All you have to do is to sign this scroll."

As Bobby said this, the curtain came down and everyone crowded around Pampas to congratulate him on his victory. Pampas looked relieved as he recognized that it had all been a practical joke and quickly signed the scroll. Then he took another look at the scroll and saw it contained the names of all the aircrew and that they were to have drinks on him. But Pampas, a half Maori, was not to be out done. He led us all in a Maori war dance, with many loud haka, haka, haka, much stamping of feet, and sticking out of tongues. Then he led us to the bar.

The children on board came along for their dinners just in time to see and hear the war dance. I think that confused them or even scared them a bit. However, their mothers understood and tried to explain enough of what they had seen to satisfy their young ones.

I told the whole story to Jo when I saw her that evening. She expressed amazement in the relationship Bobby had with the members of his squadron. She had been around the navy for a long time and never before had she seen the squadron leader and the aircrew so chummy. Jo suggested that Bobby's attitude and the fact he didn't lord anything over them may have been the answer of why he was so popular with the squadron. She'd heard other squadron leaders say he was irresponsible, but she believed that they were caught up in old time naval ways of thinking and acting, as well as protecting their own egos.

After dusk action stations the next night, I met Jo again and we went up to the very front of the flight deck and again stood shoulder to shoulder, each with an arm around the other's back, braced against the wind flowing up from the prow. I felt the ship beneath me was a living thing, driving through the ocean like a determined swimmer, while the strong clean ocean winds dampened our faces with salt spray. I felt very much in touch with the vitality of the world around us. I wondered if Jo did. I didn't ask. We chatted on for a while about this and that and then, after a period in which neither of us spoke, she told me how much she'd enjoyed our time together. Tomorrow, we'd be in Liverpool, so she and Alex would be off to rejoin her husband. She invited me to come visit them if we were ever in Lee.

With that she turned, kissed lightly me on the cheek and we went below, she to her quarters, I to my mine. I didn't expect to ever see her again. Probably a good thing, I thought. She was married and has a child; I was married too. I felt I'd added a very interesting new 'sister' in England, much like the girl across the street at home with whom I'd grown up, but she'd never kissed me on the cheek. In the long letter I wrote to my wife, I was very careful how I described my relationship with Jo, so that she wouldn't think it was more than it was.

The next morning, the approaches to the North Channel were obscured by fog and the Nabob anchored. Channel fever had been rife amongst the returning English, and I thought they must have felt frustrated being delayed this way, so close to home. Finally, on 5 April, we arrived in Liverpool and tied up at Gladstone Dock.

Chapter Nine

Two Gorgeous Movie Stars

The first day in Liverpool, half of the crew had shore leave. The other half was scheduled for the second day, which I knew was very much appreciated by the crew. Our sea-sick tiffie recovered as soon as we arrived in Liverpool and, other than being a bit thinner, apparently no worse for his ten days of intravenous feeding. However, our hopes that he might again have him back as the active and efficient worker that we had glimpsed in New York, vanished when, two days later, the Nabob heeled maybe one degree, as a tug helped us from our moorings on leaving Gladstone Docks. He vomited, and that continued throughout our short trip on a glassy Irish Sea to the Clyde River. We discharged him to our shore establishment in Greenoch. I felt sorry for him. He was a good worker, but he couldn't cope with his seasickness.

On the way up, one of our tiffies, who seemed to be quite upset, told me what he'd done with his 'rabbit,' a term that was used to describe gifts bought to be given to friends, current and future, when they got to the UK. On his first evening ashore, he'd met this attractive and receptive young lady. After a time, when things were going well, he'd given her one of the nylon stocking of a pair he'd bought as a rabbit. He told her that the next time he was ashore he would give her the other. He hadn't known they were going to sail again so soon, and he was wondering what to do with the one he had left. I couldn't help him.

My real disappointment on this little voyage was that our squadron flew off to HMS Handrail, the base at Macrahanish on the Isle of Mull. I was really disappointed because I was just getting to know these men, and now they were going to be gone. We returned to Liverpool for a Royal Navy refit.

But this time it was not to Gladstone Dock, but to Alexandra Pier where I learned that this refit was required to bring the Nabob up to British standards. Apparently, the Royal Navy was not satisfied with the Nabob as she was and wanted to make some changes that would take three or four weeks. Because of my experience in Halifax with British ships, I had some apprehension about this plan, but mostly because I wondered if the British really knew what they were doing. The Americans had been using ships like the Nabob both in the Atlantic and Pacific Oceans for some time and probably knew a lot more about the proper equipment for them than the British with their limited experience. But it was the British who were going to make changes to this American-built ship, to the tune of three or four weeks. To calm down, I decided to visit downtown Liverpool.

The long streetcar trip from the dockyards on the Mersey River into the city gave me an opportunity to see the extent of the damage caused by the previous relentless Nazi bombing. I saw that huge areas had been destroyed, then cleared and now lay as empty fields. Particularly impressive was the area sector around the recently completed Liverpool Cathedral, whose tower had just been finished in 1942 and already known as one of the great buildings of the twentieth century. Around this apparently undamaged cathedral, not a building was standing. When I stepped through the door I said what I heard what others had also said when they came in: "Wow."

It was breathtaking; a scene such as I had never even imagined before. The awesome scale of the world's highest and widest Gothic arches enclosed a magnificent space with its beautiful stained-glass windows. I stood quietly and listened for fifteen awe-struck minutes to an orchestra practicing and was overwhelmed by the acoustics. I didn't take time to climb the 330-foot tower to see its magnificent view. Nor did I hear the peal of the thirteen Bartlett bells that I learned required a leader and seven assistants to play. I hoped I would another time.

After that I walked up to the city center and saw the famous Royal Liver building (an address I knew, but didn't previously know was famous), but I'd known as housing the office of my father's British lumber broker. I made no effort to visit him, for I remembered vividly how much I disliked the man. Lord (I never could remember his name) had dinner at our home one time. He had impressed me as one who looked down on us 'Colonials,' as he called us. He acted so superior, yet I thought his table manners were atrocious. Somehow, he seemed to strain his soup through his great mustache, making loud slurping noises. As he put his spoon to his lips, some of the soup dribbled down over his vest. I remembered no redeeming qualities. Probably nouveau riche, I had decided as a teenage boy.

Most of the time walking up Hanover Street, I'd just gawked, looking in any window that appeared interesting and how much things cost in pound, shillings and pence; money entirely foreign to me. One time I noticed a woman on the other side of the street who seemed to be doing much the same as I. My immediate impression of her was that she fitted my concept of a typical English housewife, fairly tall and lean, an unstylish hairdo, dressed in woolen tweeds, both jacket and skirt, brown walking shoes and carrying a brown leather but otherwise a nondescript handbag. A little time later, I noticed her again, now some distance behind me. Something in a window on the other side of the street attracted me, so I crossed the street to get a better view of it. Right next door there was an entrance with an overhead sign that said "Rooms to Rent." I thought nothing of it until a few minutes later I felt a nudge—much more than just an accidental touching. Looking around, there was my most respectable English woman just about to enter the door. She was looking at me with a slight lift her head towards the door and a look on her face that clearly said "Are you interested?" I kept on walking. But the event had an impact, for I decided that from then on, I would be more careful about deciding about anyone's occupation might be by the way they looked or the costume they were wearing.

That night I found that a course in Aviation Medicine was about to begin at the Royal Naval Air Station (RNAS) at Eastleigh, near Southampton. This was a medical field I knew nothing about and needed to know if I was to look after our aircrew adequately. Also, I wanted to be able to talk to the aircrew using a language we both knew and gain their confidence by showing them that I knew what I was talking about. I expected this course would supply me with that kind of know-how I needed to be an effective flight surgeon in my private war against Hitler. The prospect of being able to take this course excited me.

Walter was enthusiastic, the captain acquiesced, arrangements were completed, and I was on my way the next weekend.

During the day-long trip to Eastleigh (near Southampton, I was told), I wondered how I would be treated by the Royal Navy. I'd read extensively as a child and youth how Canadian troops had been used in the last war. An outstanding example was how our Princess Patricia Light Infantry battalion, consisting entirely of McGill University students, then recognized as being the brightest of our Canadian youth, always being used as 'shock' troop, with difficult assignments, resulting in their personnel having to be replaced three times. I'd also read of comparable colonial treatment that Indian, New Zealand, and Australian troops had received in the Dardenelles.

The few months I spent in Halifax had been long enough to learn that at the beginning of the war, the British Admiralty had again demanded that our Canadian Navy be under its control. That it didn't happen was because our Prime Minister, MacKenzie King, would not accede. He remembered the arrogant way the British had behaved toward the Canadians during the Great War, and he defended our sovereignty. But as virtually all of our senior naval officers had received their training in the Royal Navy, we needed an ongoing effort to maintain the separation. Even so, I'd learned that in this war, Royal Navy ships received the newest radar and similar new equipment first, while often our Canadian ships got inferior equipment or none at all. This happened despite an agreement to the contrary. Now I was going to be attached to this arrogant navy for three weeks. I wondered what it was going to be like.

Arriving in Eastleigh in the evening, I hailed a taxi and went immediately to the Royal Navy Air Station. It didn't look too impressive, as it merely consisted of a number of one-story wooden buildings, partially protected by earthen embankments and arranged parallel to a large rectangular grass field, which I soon learned was the landing field. On the other side were two large black buildings, a factory for building Spitfires, I was told. I checked in and was assigned a room. The night passed quietly except for the sound of many airplanes flying overhead. I knew they were incessantly attacking the German forces, just across the English Channel, not that many miles away. At last, I was getting close to the real war.

Breakfast the next morning presented me with my first introduction to the ambience and the idiosyncrasies of the Royal Navy. Entering a large dining room, I saw rows of long tables with white table cloths. Most of the places were already taken by capless officers of various ranks, busily eating their breakfasts, simultaneously reading their newspaper, supported by wooden racks placed immediately in front of each reader-eater. No murmur of conversation was to be heard, only the sound of knives, forks and spoons clanging on china plates. After inspecting the situation, I found an unoccupied place between two breakfasters and said. "Hello," right and left. No response. With hardly daring a sideways glance, I ate my breakfast and became another of the reader-eaters. It was not an atmosphere that I wanted to endure.

Near the post breakfast coffee room was shelf space where everyone checked their caps. I was very aware of how new and unsalty my cap badge was, and I did something that I have always regretted. One stacked cap had a very used badge. I slipped that badge off and replaced it with my shiny new one. Then, complete with guilty conscience, I joined the rest of the officers for some very bitter coffee; it had lots of chicory, I was told.

Conversation was allowed in the coffee room and went on full blast, but already I'd decided to limit my exposure to this atmosphere; I simply felt I didn't belong. After lunch, I managed to borrow a bicycle from one of the more friendly types. He even allowed me to keep it for the entire three weeks I was to be there. This bicycle had three speeds; the kind that I'd dreamed about as a youngster, but in the Depression years, such a bike was more expensive than my family or anyone else in our town could afford. It didn't take me long to find out that biking on a three-speed here was a lot easier than on my old one-speed back home.

Before class that morning I met the WREN (Women's Royal Naval Service) officer in charge, Lieutenant Irene Marshall. She was an attractive, dark haired vivacious young woman, whose green eyes fascinated me. She had the ability to treat each of us students as individuals, always with a good sense of humor and yet firmly, accepting no nonsense from anyone, no matter their rank. She distributed a syllabus entitled "Air Medical School." In it was a day by day, actually hour by hour, listing of the times and hours and titles of each activity and/or activity for the next three weeks. I thought the program outlined was very extensive and comprehensive, using lectures, movies, actual flying, a decompression chamber, even a wet dinghy drill. The six other students, all British, seemed very pleasant and co-operative, but less assertive than my Canadian classmates. I never got to know them very well because I didn't live on base, nor did they learn what a Canadian doctor was like, at least not this one, but perhaps they thought they did. I wasn't especially interested in getting to know these doctors socially; I was more interested in learning the material in this course and what the local British were like.

After class that first afternoon, mostly introductory movies, I pedaled into Southampton and then out the Winchester road. I found it very invigorating riding around and feeling so very carefree. In due course, I arrived at the village of Chandler's Ford and saw a small hotel, called the Hut. Suddenly it occurred to me that this might be a more pleasant place to spend the next three weeks than the living quarters at the Royal Naval Air Station. Also, it would also give me an opportunity to meet more of the local citizens; I could meet Navy types anytime. I was delighted when I found I could rent a small but adequate room on the second story. It had a stone floor, and its window looked out on a nearby field where the six guns of an anti-aircraft battery gave evidence of having been there for some time. To the left, fifty feet away, a tall pole supported an air raid siren.

After registering, I pedaled over to the base, told Irene what I had done (she looked amused), picked up my stuff, and returned to the Hut for dinner.

After dinner, I looked further around my new abode. On the ground floor, I found that beside the reception desk and the dining room, there was a kitchen and two pubs. I learned that the patrons of the larger of the pubs entered from the street and were mostly villagers and British and American soldiers. It was open only two nights a week. There, the call "Time, Gentlemen Please" occurred about 2130. Its only form of physical activity was centered about several dart boards; they were busy most of the time.

The other, and much smaller pub, had an entrance from the lobby. The smell of five war year's accumulation of cigarette smoke, spilt beer, and various spirits that had permeated the carpets and sofas, and essentially everything in the room. It was strong, but I got used to it. Its clientele were house guests and a few privileged individuals from the village. That contact with the British people was very attractive to me, for in the evenings these pubs provided me with the life stories of these new acquaintances.

The next afternoon, our course provided its first really interesting learning experience. The subject was anoxia, chronic and acute. Four of us went into a decompression chamber so we could see for ourselves how anoxia would affect us. We put on earphones; a microphone was mounted in the chamber.

The director of the experiment assured us that with both the hearing and voice channels, we would be in constant communication. We were given paper and pencils and instructed to write things, anything, such as our name or letters to our wives. I found this comforting that we only had to do those simple things.

Two students wore oxygen masks from the beginning, but another student named Peter Monk and I did not. When the air pressure had been reduced to equivalent of 18,000 feet, I began to feel air hungry. One of my masked colleagues said of me, "Look, he's getting cyanotic, see that." With further decompression, I apparently became quite upset with the director because he insisted I was no longer writing to my wife, but to a girlfriend. At 25,000 feet, I apparently was no longer functioning rationally, and my two oxygen-wearing colleagues revived me by placing an oxygen mask over my mouth and nose. Later, this was called chronic anoxia. We then "descended" to the equivalent of 21,000 feet. At that level, the two who had been wearing oxygen masks until now removed them. Within a minute or so, they became deeply cyanotic and collapsed; we saw with our own eyes the effect of acute anoxia as compared to the chronic anoxia we had experienced. The whole experiment lasted a little less than two hours. For the next day or so, I battled both exhaustion and depression.

Two days later, Friday, I had a flight with what was called a 'tame' pilot in a Fairey Fulmar, an aluminum-sheathed aircraft stressed to withstand high-gravity turns. I was to experience G forces. He put the aircraft through a series of tight turns as I watched an instrument attached to the top of the instrument panel directly in front of me that recorded the G (gravity). Initially the turns were mild, but gradually they became tighter. With each succeeding one, the indicator showed higher and higher G. At 5 1/2 G, I could barely move my arms; I was told they were almost as heavy as molten iron. Apparently, I was very resistant, because even at 7 G, I still could see the indicator and never did totally black out. It was interesting, but not especially pleasant. Afterwards, the pilot told me about the new Frank Flying Suit, a Canadian anti-G suit that had just become available. It prevented the wearer from blacking out. Incidentally, he told me that (true or not) this was the then secret Canadian anti-G suit or its prototype that Sir Fredrick Banting, the discoverer of insulin, may have been taking to the UK when he was the only one killed in a mild crash in a Newfoundland swamp. He died because he refused to put on his seat belt.

In the second week, the subjects of our classes were not as exciting, but still very important, such as how to cross-match for blood transfusions (which I already knew and had done) how to establish fitness for flying examinations, how to care and maintain special equipment such as dinghies and Mae Wests, how to treat burns, and the principles of fire-fighting. On Friday, I spent much of the afternoon flying in Tiger Moths at low altitudes around the area. This gave me a wonderful opportunity to see a little of how the army was arranging its forces for the invasion of France. Looking down, I could see the many local wooded areas that were totally filled with tents and miscellaneous military paraphernalia, the ditches filled with what appeared to be bombs, the roads leading to even small south coast harbours and finally their jetties, lined with tanks. There seemed to be no empty spaces. I thought that the German air force must have been in poor shape if they couldn't drop any bombs here. They wouldn't have been able to miss.

One Saturday evening I set off to visit Jo Dewsbury and her husband at Lee-On-Solent, a trip that required both train and bus rides. When I got off the train at Fareham to wait for the bus, I noticed a Jaguar parked about half way down the car park with two women standing beside it. I'd always thought that Jaguars had the best design of all cars, so I walked down to look at it up close. However, when I got near I saw that the two women were both young and absolutely beautiful. Immediately I forgot all about the Jag. Attracted and curious,

I walked over and introduced myself. They responded in kind, and I discovered that they were Joan Fontaine and her sister, Olivia de Haviland. We made small talk for maybe ten minutes and then Olivia told me that they were going to have a smashing party the next weekend. She invited me to join them.

I was overwhelmed. I was invited to a party with not one, but two, gorgeous movie stars. One was already an Oscar winner and the other surely soon would be. I wondered what the party would be like. Who the other guests might be? How glamorous would it all be? Then I became acutely aware that I was married and while a one evening party might be okay, one lasting a whole weekend might not be appropriate. So, after what probably was a very long pause, I declined the invitation and got on the now waiting bus. We hadn't travelled a hundred yards when I wished I'd agreed. I loved Anne, and I could remain faithful even at a weekend party. But it was too late. I have regretted that decision ever since.

On the following Monday, I had my first of five more flights in a Tiger Moth, a biplane configured to have single seats, one mostly under the top wing, the other about two feet behind it. This was the same kind of aircraft in which I'd had my first flight in Charlottetown in 1937. Both seats were equipped with all the equipment needed to fly the plane, such as a rudder pedal, a joy stick and an instrument panel. A very simple plane, it had long been used to teach students to fly and that was its purpose that day. I was the student and I was very anxious, even though I long had wanted to be able to fly. My pilot, sitting in the front seat, was experienced, or so I was told, and after having already flown with him several times, I had no doubt of that.

After we were airborne for a while, he called back to me that it was time for me to take over and fly the plane.

With some anxiety, I agreed.

"Just keep the plane pointed toward the horizon. That's all you have to do."

That sounded simple enough. I took the joy stick in my hand and started looking for the horizon. It wasn't that easy. The sky was a leaden grey and, so far as I could see, so was the land. There was no way could I see the horizon in all that grey. The real danger was in the plane hitting the ground, so if I made sure that I was at least aiming this bird above where I thought the horizon might be, everything should be fine. It wasn't so. Little by little, the aircraft began to shake, steadily becoming worse. Then the pilot's voice came over the intercom that we were getting close to a stall. He took over to show me what would happen if we continued with this speed and angle of flight.

Sure enough, we shuddered almost to a stop and then fell away in a spin. Though I was initially afraid, I had confidence in the pilot, and in that moment, I hoped that it was justified. It was, for in due course he pulled out nicely. It was exciting, not that I wanted him to repeat it. At lower altitudes, I could see how a spin would be bad business. But he took my enthusiasm for his skill as an encouragement to demonstrate his ability to make this aircraft do tricks. I wasn't certain that was a good idea, but I wasn't really in a position to protest. We experienced loop de loops; Immelmann turns; dives; and spins; turns at rates one, two, three, and four; and basically everything in his playbook. I loved it all, but the loop de loop was my favorite. We were flying level when suddenly we were going straight up, then he inverted the plane so I was upside down, my body pressed against the seat. I looked down. There was no airplane between me and the ground. That didn't last long for the plane went on to complete the circle. What a thrill! But I now regret that the pilot did not settle me down after the original spin and really encouraged me to fly the plane properly. I think he was probably tired of flying guys like me around and decided to just have some fun instead. Maybe he thought that was all I was interested in.

Across the field from our Flight Surgeon course huts were two large black windowless buildings. I'd been told that they were two of the many facilities scattered throughout the country where Spitfires were built. Almost every afternoon about 1500, two new Spits rolled out onto the airfield to begin their life of flight; I became totally spellbound. Then, as these beautiful airplanes took off and flew what looked like straight up to begin their test flights, I imagined I was with them, sitting on a wing. When the two pilots began to dog fight them at 360 miles per hour and more through a series of rolls, dives, and spins, all directly overhead, I was still on one or other of the planes, sometimes feeling like a bird, at other times fighting the G, always totally thrilled. I saw the progress of a Spitfire through the sky as effortless, as if it were simply riding the breeze and the sound of its Griffon engine being a whisper or a simple sound track. I was enjoying the thrill of unfettered flight, enthralled.

It was in those moments that I understood why Bobby Bradshaw, on seeing the unattended Hurricane, the Battle of Britain companion of the Spit, on the tarmac of a desert air force base, would impulsively run over, get in its cockpit, take off and test it in actual air combat. I'd like to think that had I had his skills, I'd have done the same thing.

But one afternoon I was standing by the airfield an hour or so after watching another Spitfire spectacular, I had the saddening experience of seeing an American Thunderbolt start flying across the field. The pilot obviously didn't see the barrage balloon or the wire tethered to it. It wrapped around his port wing, just as it was supposed to and the aircraft began its vertical plummet to earth. I looked away. It made a huge hole at least fifteen to twenty feet deep. The pilot did not survive.

Chapter Ten

Everyday English People

In the three weeks I stayed at the Hut, I enjoyed getting to know these everyday English people, such as the town people who were privileged to come into the private bar. Despite what they'd been through, they were uniformly pleasant and cheerful. Most conversations were about the soon-to-be invasion, but not a single one ever let slip any information that would have been useful to the enemy, were I one. I was the only short-term guest; the others in the hotel all seemed to be more or less permanent. Two older women called Betty and Gladys were especially outgoing, so I had several long conversations with them. Eventually I invited them to come have a drink in the private bar. They both ordered pink gins.

Together they told me their stories, especially about their work as part of the Spitfire team. They were part of a close-knit and devoted group who truly loved this warm, friendly plane designer named George Mitchel, and they were devastated when they learned that he had colon cancer. He'd died in 1937. They'd been with him at Supermarine way back in the early twenties when his emphasis was designing airplanes to win the coveted Schneider Trophy. Three of his racer float planes won, one setting a world's speed record of 357 miles per hour in 1929. Betty explained how that had led to a contract with the Air Ministry to build a fighter aircraft for the Royal Air Force. They told me about one day when they were deciding what kind of a wing they would use. Was it to be an elliptical wing? Suddenly George, not a patient man, said loudly, "I don't care what shape it is so long as we can get guns in it." Finally, a Canadian aeronautical engineer named Beverly Sheastone made the suggestion to which that they all agreed. They were all terribly saddened when their George Mitchell died, but Joseph Smith, who had been his number one assistant from the beginning, took over and devised all the more than twenty-odd modifications that were made from that time on, including substituting the Rolls Royce Griffon engine for the original Merlin. His modifications always kept the Spitfire the best fighter plane in the sky.

Betty and Gladys were proud of their beautiful Spitfires that they felt they'd had a part in building. They both had to resign their positions because of age, but they did have a wonderful, rewarding, and exciting time as a part of the Spitfire team. Sure, there were times when it was frightening, but out here, even when the Germans were bombing the hell out of Southampton, it wasn't that bad. They read many books in the air raid shelters.

With that, I bought them another round to celebrate their wonderful careers with two such amazing men. How lucky I was to have met these women. They'd been involved in the building of the more than twenty thousand of the aircraft that I'd so admired.

One of the other guests staying at the Hut was a young man named Tony. He got up early every morning and pedaled off to work, I was told, in the Spitfire factory. But when I asked him about what he did, he was mum. "I can't tell you, even if you are a naval officer," he said. What I saw was that when he returned in the afternoon, his main occupation seemed to be hanging out with the landlord's daughter, a rather hard-looking bleached blond who looked at least twenty years older than he. It turned out that he was Anthony Noel, the 5th Earl of Gainsborough, and the whisper was that he was one of those thought eligible to become the husband of Princess Elizabeth. I hoped for everyone's sake it would continue to be but a whisper.

I did my best to keep track on how the preparations for the invasion of Normandy seemed to be progressing. Peddling around on my bicycle, I saw the piles of munitions and supplies that filled the ditches. On roads leading to every jetty were long lines of tanks, mostly Shermans, already water sealed and ready for action. Some of them had gun barrels longer than the rest, with the extra length covered by camouflaged materials. From my many low-altitude flights, I saw that the woods had now become military encampments, thousands of men living in tents, getting ready. The American 1st Division, the Canadian 3rd and the British 50th all were close by, waiting, making final preparations. These men were rumored to be in the first wave. Seeing them sitting in the Hut or moving about outside, I admired and respected them, but I grieved at the same time, because I knew the reality of war. Many of them would be killed, and so many more would be wounded and maimed. Marching down the street, they looked so fit, so confident, so alert, and so vibrantly alive. I'd lift my glass to them, but I often ended up with tears running down my cheeks.

When I learned that the North Nova Scotia Highlanders, the battalion from around my home in Nova Scotia, was camped nearby at Fareham, I decided to make a visit. Taking a taxi to a village near the camp, I then walked the remaining mile or so. Our Nova Scotia flag flying at the entrance told me I was at the right place. On 6 June, it became the first Canadian flag flown in France. The guard at the entrance grilled me intensively, making sure I was who I claimed to be. Amongst the information that I told him was that Don Learmont was a friend of mine (I'd known him in college). I wasn't surprised to discover that he'd attained the rank of major. Unfortunately, Don was not at camp that day. Then I saw Bill Douglas, who I'd known since I was a child. He used to walk by our house on his way to high school. The way he walked wasn't like the others; he always marched as if he were a soldier, even all those years ago.

This visit with the Novas was rather a bittersweet experience. I was so glad to see my old friends there, looking so fit and assured, apparently quite unafraid of the future despite knowing they were going into battle on D-Day. But I had a hard time keeping cheerful; I so afraid for their futures. I didn't stay very long, unable to face the fact that the lives of so many of these men would soon be cut short by shrapnel and gunfire.

Later on, I would learn that their losses were even worse than I had feared, for just in the first sixty days, eight hundred and fifty of their officers and men were dead, wounded or missing. Only sixteen of the original members were still with the battalion.

The day after trying to visit my friends, I was back in class. About lunch time, Irene Marshall, the WREN officer who ran the program, asked me if I'd been into Southampton yet to look around. She had helped me out many times, doing such things as reminding me of a class I was about to miss, where to get a certain book that I hadn't been able to find, or how to get the train to Fareham. We'd become good friends.

When I told her I had only been to the suburbs, she suggested that we catch the bus and go check out Southampton proper. It sounded like a great afternoon. Going there, though, I realized that the venerable old city had been badly damaged.

The first time I'd gone there, I'd only seen the suburbs, so now when I was right in the city, I could see what the Germans had done to Southampton. It was shocking, even worse than Liverpool. Virtually all of the central part of the city had been destroyed by Nazi bombing earlier in the war, and by now, the debris had been almost all been removed. For blocks and blocks, this city was nothing more than large empty fields; there were not even any weeds. But one large building stood alone amongst all this emptiness, the seemingly undamaged Hotel Polygon, a 4-star establishment. In true British fashion, the old girl was still at work, calmly carrying on her business in spite of the devastation around her. That, to me, deserved some sort of recognition.

Irene suggested we go in and have afternoon tea. She'd voiced the thoughts in my head.

Tea was served in the elegant lobby. Everything seemed to be as it should be, the waitresses in their trim black dresses and white aprons. We were seated immediately, but after an appropriate interval that allowed us to get settled, our waitress approached. "Tea for two, sir?" she asked, the English accent rolling off her tongue. It was so much like what I'd seen and heard in British movies, it seemed to me as if we were in one, and that this was not real. However, I recovered quickly and gave her our orders. I'd wondered what the area about the hotel would look like from the window, so I took this moment to walk to a window and look around. In every direction, there was nothing but empty land, not even one blade of grass. Despite being surrounded by a wasteland, we were about to sip tea in this elegant hotel, whose traditionally dressed waitresses continued to provide impeccable service. It seemed to me to be a tragically beautiful metaphor for this country in general, maintaining her dignity even as she was battered by the horrors of a war unlike anything the world had ever seen before. War suspends and eliminates many of the fundamental rules of civility, society, and morality. Mild-mannered schoolteachers rack up kill counts. Instead of planning to go to college, teenagers plan to leave their mothers and cross the seas to fight an unseen enemy. Strong, fit young men who should have another fifty years ahead of them meet their ends in blood, pain, and fire.

Yet this hotel served a beautiful tea.

Afterward, Irene and I walked down to the similarly flattened dockyard area where floating in the harbour was a structure like I'd never seen before. Built on what looked was a very large caisson was a rectangular structure that looked to be about four hundred feet long, forty feet or so wide and maybe fifty feet above the waterline.

What the hell was that?

Irene didn't know, so I asked a passerby. He told us that somebody said it was called a Phoenix, and it had something to do with the invasion. That was all he knew. I didn't try to get any further information once I knew it was related to the invasion. Nobody would talk if they knew that it was in some way connected to the war. We all knew that loose lips could sink a ship, and we were all doing our part by keeping mum even when we believed we could trust the people around us. I puzzled about this strange structure, but I couldn't imagine how it could be used.

Being with my green-eyed date was very enjoyable, and she capped the afternoon by lamenting that we hadn't done this more often.

I agreed.

That night, something new happened to me. During these weeks that I stayed at the Hut, there was only one time that the air raid sirens had sounded, but nothing had happened. I'd concluded that the Germans must no longer have the ability to mount one, for it was obvious that a bomb dropped anywhere for miles around would have caused a lot of damage. However, this night there was an attack on the docks in Southampton, perhaps intended to destroy that odd structure called the Phoenix that we'd seen anchored out in the stream. I'd gone to bed about 2230, dog-tired. The air raid happened about one in the morning, I was later told. Apparently the siren just behind the hotel sounded. It didn't wake me up. All the other occupants of the hotel joined the neighboring villagers in the streets to watch the display. There was no danger to us where we were, as the target was in the

Southampton area. By all accounts, it was a brilliant show. Search-lights crisscrossed the sky and, I was also told, the ack-ack guns in the backyard added to the general uproar. Nothing awakened me; I missed it all.

Those who cannot comprehend why people would be excited or entertained by an air raid are people who haven't faced the realities of living in a war.

The next morning at breakfast, everyone was talking about what a cracking good show it had been. Everyone was talking, that is, but me. The consensus appeared to be that it was a shame I'd not seen it. The only night-time air raid I was ever in and I'd slept through it, despite an air raid siren that stood not more than fifty feet from my window and a six-gun battery of anti-aircraft that was active in a field a few hundred feet away. I hadn't heard a sound. I could hardly believe it. To say I was disappointed, was as gross an understatement as it is possible to make.

Beginning about 20 April, there had been an ever-increasing amount of military traffic on the main road that passed immediately in front of my hotel. Among the soldiers who came to the pub, tension seemed to be increasing. Incessantly, large groups of bombers and their fighter escorts flew overhead toward France. Everyone had the same question: was the long-awaited invasion of France about to occur? Was it to be on the next full moon, when the tides will be at their highest?

Then, on the first day of May, the tension was gone. I noticed it when I first awoke. Out the window I saw that the sky was blue and no cloud hid the sun. At breakfast, nobody spoke about the invasion. Military traffic on the highways was virtually non-existent. The soldiers in the pub were relaxed. I wondered what made me recognize the disappearance of the tension. I was not imagining it.

I theorized that it was just because it was our last week of classes. We had a mixture of subjects and activities, including time in the Link and Attack trainers, filling out forms, some flying, the psychology of accidents, and aircrew injuries. We followed lectures on Aeroneurosis with wet dinghy drills and preservation of life at sea. Examinations concluded our course on 5 May. They didn't amount to much, consisting of each of us giving a ten-minute talk. The subject given to me was 'Survival at Sea after Ditching.' As this was a topic that we had discussed and as I was allowed access to our books, if I so wanted, I found it to be rather fun. Actually, it was a subject I could have talked about for much longer than the time allotted.

Subsequently, I talked to Irene. She said that our instructors had difficulty in assessing me, not in my talk, which I did exceptionally well, but just in general. Apparently, I was sufficiently different from my fellow students that I confused them. Part of this, she said, was because I asked so many questions and was much more overt in expressing my opinions. Obviously, they were not use to Canadian students. However, I did get an A.

It had been a good, comprehensive course and I felt I now knew how to be a competent flight surgeon on the HMS Nabob.

Chapter Eleven

Take Up our Quarrel with the Foe

On returning to Nabob in Liverpool on 8 May, I found the refit was still in its infancy. It was not difficult to figure out why. The dockyard workers here looked like tired old men in their seventies or more, moving at a very slow pace with no sense of urgency whatsoever. Some were painting the interior of the hangar deck with brushes only two inches wide. Didn't they know there was a war on and we needed to get at it? That was my question, but the answer was that they had been offered the power brushes we carried on board, but no, they said they preferred what they'd always used. Obviously, this refit was going to take more time than planned. This was not the bustling and efficient Norfolk naval yard, where every step was brisk and every movement had a purpose.

A new pipe needed to be placed in the hangar deck, a job that required, according to the union, a crew of thirty-six. But at 0600, only thirty-five showed up. Those who had come at the correct time waited and waited, until 0730 when the thirty-sixth arrived. Then, as I watched, about six of them went to work; the rest watched. In half an hour, the job was finished and they left. I was amazed at the power this labor union possessed even in wartime. I thought that if this was true for all the unions, the British were going to have major economic troubles when the war was over.

Walter and most of the crew were on leave, and although I con-ducted Sick Call each morning, nobody was ever sick. As soon as Walter returned, I asked for and received a week's leave.

On 20 May I felt fine and proud that I now could read the English train tables as I took the train to Worcester and to visit the grave of my life-long friend, Flying Officer Gordon Hagen. I thought back to some of our times together, especially when the two of us had raised chinchilla rabbits and how disappointed we were that morning when we found all fourteen of our rabbits had been killed, eaten by some animal, probably a weasel. I remembered how worried his other close friends and I were when we learned that after he'd enlisted as a radar officer. He'd taken advantage of newly lowered sight standards and re-enlisted for pilot training. He was not a well-coordinated person, not even being able to ride a bicycle worth a damn. I had lunch with him in Montreal shortly before he sailed to the United Kingdom and asked him why he'd done it. His answer was about as I expected. Being a radar officer was well and good, but he'd wanted to be more actively fighting in this war. His patriotism and zeal for the cause were commendable, but I did wonder at the wisdom of him taking a position he was so clearly not suited for. It had come to a tragic conclusion.

With his still-grieving, very attractive girlfriend, I placed flowers on his beautifully kept grave and those of his aircrew in the cemetery in nearby Evesham. I remembered another friend from school days, Creighton Lowther, who had become a National Hockey League hockey player, then a; RCAF pilot. He hadn't returned from the first Allied 1000-plane bombing attack on Berlin.

That night, while staying at his RAF air station (Honeybourne), I felt unusually tired. The next morning, I wasn't as spry as usual, and by the time I'd hitched hike all the way to Eastleigh to have dinner with Irene, I wasn't worth much. My attempts at conversation were lacking in spirit and I felt physically exhausted.

But the next morning, not feeling well, I still was determined to visit Lieutenant Norman Fraser, a close friend in college days. With some difficulty because of the heightened security, I was able to find out that his engineering unit (the 6th Field Park), a unit of the Canadian Army's 2nd Division, was near Folkestone on the east coast, quite a long distance away. Despite feeling worse each day, I managed to get an extraordinary overview of the preparations for the invasion as I travelled along the south coast. A lot had changed in the past three weeks. The number of military vehicles on the roads had increased exponentially; the size of the canvas covered piles of munitions in the ditches had at least doubled. Near every port, large or small, miles and miles of tanks were lined up, exponentially more than what I'd seen previously. Grey canvas was draped over all unusually long barrels on the tanks, presumably to hide them from any hostile eyes in the sky. The whole scene added up to what it looked to me to be an overpowering accumulation of military might, all of which was going to have to be transported across the English Channel. What an amazing challenge it would be to move all the men and these armaments across the Channel to Normandy. The next day I got a ride in a military jeep to Normie's unit, complete with a little fever to accompany my fatigue. After dinner that evening, we drove into Canterbury and had a beer in an outdoor pub facing the badly damaged famous cathedral. Soon, the air was filled with the thunder of at least 400 warplanes heading east and subsequently returning.

Normie explained that they'd been doing this for days. The bombing was said to be in the area between Calais and Boulogne. That wasn't Normandy, so it was possible that it was for some other purpose.

When the din lessened, I told him about Gordon Hagen's death. Normie observed that it was a tragic death in a family filled with tragedy. Then he urged me to think of all the soldiers and airmen that I'd passed in the past few weeks who would be wounded or killed in the invasion. Thousands and thousands of men now alive would soon be individual tragedies, but in years to come, they'd just be the statistics of the war. I'd done much of that sort of thinking while sitting in the Hut, and here I was at it again.

After such maudlin thoughts, we needed a new topic of conversation. So I asked him when the invasion was set to occur.

Normie figured that if we had to, we could have been ready to move out tomorrow. But if we were to continue at our usual pace, it was likely to be in two weeks.

I felt even worse when at 0500 the next morning, I dragged myself on to the train to London and eventually on to Liverpool and to my bed on the Nabob that evening. The week's leave had been pretty disappointing.

The next morning, I still felt exhausted, but now I also had a persistent hacking cough and a temperature of 102. With Walter, I went to the Sick Bay. He thoroughly examined me, did a sputum culture (negative), and conducted a white blood cell count that showed I had decreased neutrophils and increased lymphocytes, which we considered to be typical of a viral infection. PO Hines took X-rays of my chest that both Walter and I agreed showed hazy infiltrates in both lungs, confirming Walter's physical examination findings. There was no doubt; the diagnosis was viral pneumonia. For that we had no medicines. I decided to stay on board, because I was afraid that if I went to the Navy Hospital on shore, I might be replaced and I was determined to stay on the Nabob. Walter agreed.

The first two weeks passed in a daze with high temperatures, but by third week I began to feel much better. It was then that Walter told me about one party they'd had in the wardroom one night. The chiefs and petty officers were guests in the wardroom along with Viscount Leverhulme, the son of the founder of the Unilever Company, his daughter, and Admiral Evans, said to be the most decorated officer in the Royal Navy. Back in 1917, when Evans was captain (D) of the destroyer HMS Broke, they attacked and sunk three German destroyers. The next year he was involved in one of the first combined operations raid in naval history. That was when the Navy attacked Zeebrugge in Belgium on St. George's Day (23 April) and HMS Vindictive responded to the famous ancient British battle cry from Commander Keyes, "St George for Merrie England," with "May we give the dragon's tail a damned good twist." It was significant Naval history, but possibly because I still had little energy, it didn't seem very interesting to me.

Just a few days later, a Red Cross Blood Unit came on board to accept blood donations; virtually all of our crew volunteered. When I learned of this, I realized that if they were collecting fresh blood it meant that the invasion of Normandy must be very near. I remembered that Normie had said they'd be ready on 5 or 6 June.

D-Day did come a few days later, 6 June, 1944. While recognizing that this was a historic day, I grieved, thinking of all the strapping, confident young men I'd seen and talked with in those weeks when I was staying at the Hut and especially my friends in the North Novas of Canada's 3rd Division, the American 1st Division and of the British 50th. I knew, and I'm sure they knew, that they were all going to be in the first wave on D-Day. They would have known that they would suffer heavy casualties, many of them giving their limbs and lives. It's no easy thing for a young man to walk into certain death; they must have believed strongly in our mission to rid the world of the horrors of Nazism.

Still weak from my illness, lying in my bed as I tried to process the necessary horror of what was happening, my thoughts went back to Dr. John McCrae's seminal poem.

IN FLANDERS FIELDS

We are the Dead.
Short days ago
We lived, felt dawn, saw sunset glow,
Loved and were loved, and now we lie in
In Flanders fields.
Take up our quarrel with the foe:
To you from failing hands we throw
The torch; be yours to hold it high.
If ye break faith with us who die
We shall not sleep, though poppies grow
in Flanders fields.

I felt as if these words, written by another Canadian physician, were a direct command, and I was relieved that at least I was in a position ready to help in a small way to carry them out.

During the following ten days, I still had little energy to follow more than cursory reports of the invasion. Even by 16 June, I had not been out of bed for more than an hour or so at a time. But when I learned we were sailing the next day and I was feeling reasonably well, I decided that I could easily convalesce on a sea voyage. It was our last day on land, so I got dressed and shakily walked over to the street car line and set off for down town Liverpool. By the time I arrived, I was feeling very weak. Seeing a cinema where I could sit down, I decided to see whatever movie was showing. When I came out, I felt much better and walked across to the Adelphi Hotel. There was not much doing in the lobby so I left, but as I was descending the stairs to the street, an attractive WAAF officer was coming up. Impulsively, I asked her if she knew Marjorie Wallace, the WAAF officer that had been my patient in Montreal the previous summer. Whether she did or not, I don't know, but she said she did and that was enough. So this lady and I decided to go to the Officer's Club that was at street level in the hotel. Then as more officers came in, we invited anyone alone to join us. Before long, we had grown to about a dozen, all Air Force or Navy. With the stimulus of a few drinks, happy conversations soon occurred, finally leading to making plans for a big party for the weekend. Of course, I knew we were sailing the next day, but I couldn't tell anyone that. It also meant that I had to enter freely into the planning. That made it fun, but embarrassing at the same time. The party was to start the next afternoon at one of the girl's apartment and last to Sunday night. Everyone said what they would bring in the way of booze and food. It really sounded like it would be a great party and I hoped that those who managed to make it would have a good time. Finally, it became about 2030, and we had to break up. Six of us, three of each gender, were all going to the streetcar depot, so off we went happily down the sidewalk, laughing and singing and holding hands and making every person we met, even police officers, walk under the loops of our joined hands. We were just like a bunch of children, any problems or worries forgotten. At the depot, we said good-bye, and all took different streetcars. I knew that we unlikely were ever to see one another again, but that we'd had a great time together that evening.

I felt alive again.

Chapter Twelve

A Hair-Raising Responsibility

It was 17 June, and, knowing we were going to sail within hours, I went to the Sick Bay first thing to make sure nobody needed medical care. There was only one patient, one of our SBAs, the same SBA that had a problem with the stocking when we first arrived. He said he was very tired, and when I took his temperature it was 105. I examined him from head to toe and found no abnormalities. I had Walter check him too, and he agreed. Then I remembered the time when I was an intern and had developed a similar fever after working for five days without sleep until exhausted. My patient had not been off the ship that long, but I was struck by the similarities of the fevers and lack of other symptoms or signs. So I asked him what he'd been doing the previous day. Little by little the story came out. Over the weeks in Liverpool, he and three of his friends had struck up very friendly relationships with two women and their daughters from Blackpool. Knowing that we were going to sail today and not knowing when, or if, they'd be back, they decided to have a special night. They set up a system so that a bell would ring every hour, signaling it was time to change partners. It was to go on all night, but my patient was the only one who lasted until dawn.

My prescription was simple. Sleep.

I had thought that such sexual activities as this lived only in the world of fantasy. But here it was, in real life. I could hardly believe what he'd told me. On the other hand, I suppose I shouldn't have been too shocked, because one of the duties all of us officers had was to censor the mail of the non-commissioned men. About a dozen of our crew had chosen me as their censor, and I regularly received their mail to inspect. What I found that was remarkable, even astounding, was the difference in their letters to their wives and to their girlfriends; if they were married, most had both. If the writer's descriptions were to be believed, those in my tiffie's sexual group were but amateurs.

After I thought I had the SBA settled, I went to talk with Walter to get an account of what had gone on while I was ill. Amongst the items that he told me about was Captain Lay's speech to the ship's company, which, of course, I hadn't heard. The captain had said that being in harbour for more than two months was both "fortunate and unfortunate." It was unfortunate because we missed being involved in the invasion of southern France. an action that many of the crew had hoped for. But that wouldn't have happened anyway, because we had already been allocated to the Commander-in-Chief, Western Approaches, as a Trade Escort Carrier. Fortunately, in these weeks, all the latest gadgets for offensive warfare had been added, although he didn't mention any details. He also said that the anti-aircraft armament had been greatly improved, and that we now had fourteen pairs of twin 'power-worked' Oerlikons, plus six single Oerlikons on improved mountings. This amounted to an increase of seven barrels on our Oerlikon armament and more efficient mountings on some of them.

I wondered what 'power-worked' meant and whether the Mark 14 gyro automatic tracking devices mounted on the Oerlikons, so greatly prized by the Americans, were still intact or were we back to the 'guess-and-good luck' gunsights the Royal Navy had been using on other ships.

The captain had commented that everyone had had a bit of leave and that many officers had taken extremely important courses, such as Fire-fighting, Damage Control, Gunnery, Torpedo, but Lay apparently said nothing about my course in Aviation Medicine, unless he included it under Air Technical Courses. Finally, he said that we were going to start our work-ups on the seventeenth, at the end of which some admiral would inspect us. That meant, I assumed, that if we passed the admiral's inspection, we would become an escort carrier in the North Atlantic. That I would like.

He hadn't mentioned it, but I'd heard that our radar had been updated. This was understandable, because at that time British radar was said to be more advanced than American, so to have incorporated the latest advances made sense. I think HDFD (High Frequency, Direction Finding) was also added.

A Jeep had been placed at our disposal when we first arrived in Liverpool, and Guy Jobin, one of our top gunners, was in charge of it. After a time, I noticed that when the captain went ashore he didn't use it. I asked Guy about that. He explained that the captain had tried once, the first day we were in Liverpool, telling Guy that he wanted to drive because 'he knew Liverpool so well.' But Guy, being the one responsible for the Jeep, had had to tell him he couldn't. After that, he never again needed the use of the Jeep. That didn't surprise Guy, because while they were in Vancouver, he'd seen the captain have his own British-made Rover put on board the Nabob just before they sailed. It even had a British license.

Lay had brought his transportation with him.

The captain of a ship had a great deal of power.

We had to leave the assigned Jeep behind when we left Liverpool, but because having our own Jeep was such a great convenience, we all felt it needed to be replaced. So when we were leaving the same port a few days later, the same Jeep, unattended, just happened to be parked on the wharf right beside our ship. Just as we began to pull away, I and some other of the crew, watched in amazement, as our portside derrick, acting as if on its own, reached down and deftly lifted that Jeep into the Nabob's friendly environs. It was quite extraordinary. Our Jeep safely tucked away, we cast aside our mooring, angled into the Mersey River and headed into the Irish Sea.

By this time, I felt that I was somewhat caught up with everyone's news, like where they'd gone and what they'd done on the courses they'd taken and what they'd done on leave. Nobody seemed to have had the variety of experiences that I'd had, but that was all in the past. Now I felt excited by both the prospect of the coming intense work-up and getting better acquainted with the members of the squadron.

During the last two months, the arresting cables had been changed. Previously about one half inch in diameter; they had been replaced by wires whose diameter I judged was three quarters of an inch. I wondered why the Royal Navy would do this, maybe because the Avenger was such a big aircraft. I wondered if the US Navy had done the same thing, or if this was just the Royal Navy. The hydraulics were now so much slower retracting the wires (now so much heavier) after they'd been extended by the landing of an Avenger. One thing was obvious: it was going to take a longer time to land our planes. That would mean sailing in a straight line for a longer time. But I, a flight surgeon, was the only one who voiced such concerns and they fell on non-responding ears.

About 1500, we were off the mouth of the Clyde River when I saw our squadron swoop down over us and begin lining up to land. What a welcome sight! I counted eleven; one aircraft was missing. I soon learned the distressing news that it was Sub-Lieutenant Lord with his navigator Sub-Lieutenant Thwaites and tail-gunner LA Winder who were missing. This was the same crew that, upon witnessing their flying between Norfolk and New York, I'd felt that the pilot was extremely talented, but had left himself no room for error. Apparently, on an exercise early in June, the squadron had been recalled to base because of dense fog. In doing so, Lord had made the mistake of turning to starboard instead of port and so had crashed into a mountain on the Isle of Mull. I didn't know any of them, but it was evident that everyone in the squadron felt deeply about losing Lord and his crew.

Before the planes landed, I saw that three wide black bands alternating with white ones had been painted on the wings of all the planes. These, I soon learned, were now common to all allied aircraft. Invasion stripes, I called them. But to me they also meant that the war was getting closer. I felt a tinge of excitement.

In the few weeks I'd been with them in Norfolk and New York, I got to know only a few of the squadron members, and now two months had passed since I'd seen any of them. My intention was to become friends with all of them. It would take time, but I thought that with the Flight Surgeon's course at Eastleigh, I was prepared. The aircrew's ready room was not far from the place on the runway where I'd chosen to stand when the aircraft were coming in to land, and close to my emergency medical care site, but somehow, I didn't feel that I could just walk in. I still felt that I was an intruder. Yet it was obviously the place where the aircrews were to be found and likely would be in a relaxed mood. I chose to let my relationship with them grow spontaneously in the course of my daily activities, and I began dropping into the ready room with increasing frequency and having chats with the crew.

During this work-up period, we sailed up and down the Irish Sea from the Mull of Kintyre to the Isle of Man. I saw that island so many times that I began to wonder how I could get ashore to see some of their short-tailed cats, but I never did. In the late afternoons or early evenings, we anchored either in the Tail of the Bank opposite Gouroch or in Belfast Lough, frequently near Bangor. There was a special reason for this latter site, I learned. It so happened that a golf course came almost down to the shore. Captain Lay was a golfer. Occasionally I'd see him and some of his golfing companions board his gig and head for the golf club. Often, I wondered how he and his fellow golfers were going to get their equipment from his boat to the shore. It was another month before I found out.

On all of the days and nights when there was flying, I stood in my chosen position in the catwalk by the first arrestor wire, watching aircraft as they took off or as they came in to land under Gavin Waite's (the batsman) magical direction. Go higher, go lower, go faster, and go slower—all these directions to the pilots just by changing the position of his bats. It was a hair-raising responsibility, and I wondered why anyone would want to do it. Gavin, a Kiwi (New Zealander), later told me that he used to be a pilot, but somehow, he'd gotten into his head that his left wing was always low, even though he could see it wasn't. That finished his piloting days. His journey from there to batsman, I never discovered.

Aiding Gavin's job was Alex Callander. As the planes were coming in to land, Callander had to report to Gavin whether the aircraft's tail hook, that extended from the tail to catch an arrestor wire, and the wheels and wing flaps were down. One time when he'd called all these things in order, the aircraft landed on the deck, but didn't slow down and continued into the barrier. The captain wanted to know why and called Callander up to the bridge. He simply reported, "The tail hook was down, sir, but it got pulled out on number three arrestor wire."

Every once in a while, we had a little prang (a minor accident) sometimes related to the weather, others for a variety of reasons such as pilot error, all of them causing me immediate anxiety until I was sure the crew was all right. On 26 June, Sub-Lieutenant Watson swung over to the port side after he landed and finished with one wing over the edge of the deck. Three days later it was Sub-Lieutenant Batten's turn. He came in too high, took a wave-off, but his hook caught in the barrier and pulled him down on a plane parked on the other side. His propeller chewed off the tail and a wing of that aircraft. Sub-Lieutenant Stevens had a turn too, a day or so later. He skidded while taxiing up the flight deck forward of the barrier and went partly over the side, resting on the walkway on the port side. His plane was considerably damaged.

That these minor accidents or worse could occur at any moment kept me always on the alert. I had Don Cash show me the switches to turn off in the cockpit after a crash if the pilot was disabled, so I made it a point to be one of the first persons to most of these prangs, ready to look after the aircrew.

The weather was often unfavorable, resulting in many planned exercises being cancelled or curtailed or postponed until a later time. These included submarine detection exercises and oiling another ship at sea.

It was during this time that both Walter and I had noticed that one of our tiffies had become a little sloppy. So when he failed to give one of our patients with gonorrhea his 0300 dose of sulfadiazene, we decided to charge him with this error. However, the captain took this very seriously, saying it was "a failure to carry out a superior officer's order in wartime at sea and so was punishable by death." This was not what we had in mind. We just wanted a slap on the wrist, like cancelling a one day's leave. Now the problem was ours or, rather, Walter's. He took over and what he did, I never knew, but our tiffie was back on duty the next day, much more attentive to the details of his duties.

After two weeks or so of almost daily watching the different pilots land their aircraft, I knew that virtually all of them were very competent, but some were a little more consistent than the others. Fred Batten was the only one I worried about. One of the best was Bill Black. At six feet one, he was one of the tallest of the group, which allowed him a full range of vision, and being a little older and already a registered pharmacist, very mature. His landings especially impressed me. He began them from a way behind the ship, much farther than any of the others and brought his plane in at a gradually descending rate. I understood that was difficult. In virtually all his landings, he caught the first wire.

One morning after breakfast, I told how much I'd like to take a ride with him. He invited me to do so that very afternoon.

Therefore, that afternoon I climbed into his aircraft, and tail gunner Stocker showed me how to get into the air-gunners ball turret, where I was cramped, but had an unobstructed view. I did wonder how I would ever get out of it in hurry, parachute and all. Bill was seated in the pilot's seat ahead of me with his observer, Sub-Lieutenant Dunbar, behind him. Stocker stayed behind on the Nabob to make more room for me. Starting at the stern of the flight deck, Bill revved the engine up to full revolutions, released the brakes and we began to roll straight down the center line. Picking up speed seemed to take forever. I reminded myself that we did have fifteen knots of wind speed and fifteen knots of ship speed, but when we passed by the island, I felt that I could run faster than the speed we were going. Was it really going to be going fast enough to get airborne? But the end of the deck did come and then disappeared behind us.

We were airborne. I was both relieved and thrilled.

Soon, we joined up with the two other members of his flight and flew in precise formations. I was surprised that sometimes our port wing was only a few feet above the starboard wing of the plane to our left. Was this usual? Was it dangerous? Everyone seemed to be doing it. It was, indeed, a very tight formation. I got out my eight-millimetre movie camera and shot some film. From five thousand feet, the Nabob looked like a toy. It seemed impossible that we were going to land on that. Then we detached from the others and did a few mild aerobatics, but nothing like the Tiger Moth pilot had done. Bill was always very much in control.

After what seemed a very few minutes, but was really an hour, Bill informed us that we were going to go land. The Nabob gradually grew larger. Then I could see the 77 painted on her flight deck and, yes, it was going to be a big enough platform to land on.

I'd watched him land so often that I had little concern, but now I was watching Bill up close just to see how he did it. I saw how intensely he concentrated on what he was doing, how steady and smooth his movements were the whole time. I then looked at Gavin and noted that he kept his bats in 'the steady as you go' position all the way until finally he drew his hand across his neck, the signal to cut the engine. Momentarily, there was just a little jerk as our hook caught the arrestor wire. We caught the first one, of course.

I'd had a great trip and had experienced for myself what flying in an Avenger was like. I thought it very important for me to have made this flight. I now knew what it was like to fly under these circumstances, to actually feel and see what my pilots had to contend with. It made me feel a little closer to all the aircrews. All of them knew about it and seemed to treat me with a little more respect after that flight.

Chapter Thirteen

Pulling, Not Pushing

Much to our dismay, the Nabob had an engine breakdown about the middle of July, which was apparently not unusual in this type of ship. That put us alongside the wharf in Belfast for repair, just when many of us, including myself, had been hoping that we'd be involved in the invasion of southern France. That put the kibosh to that, but it gave me the opportunity to visit the nearby USS Houston. This ship was the newly built replacement for the previous cruiser by the same name that had been sunk by the Japs in 1942 in the Battle of the Java Sea. I thought it was a fine-looking cruiser. So I went over to see her close up and to visit the medical staff, who received me warmly. They gave me several very useful medical instruments, especially an exophthalmometer with which I could examine the interior of eyes. They also invited me to lunch. The food was excellent, but what really impressed me were the long tables covered by stark white tablecloths and with black-uniformed servers wearing white aprons. It was certainly not what we were used to on the Nabob. They told me that the servers became integral part of gun crews in battles.

Noticing that this was a dry ship, I asked one of the medical officers what they did for liquor. As they didn't have a bar, they had to buy it while ashore and bring it to the cabins. As they paid ninety cents for two cartons of cigarettes, it was easy to trade a bottle of gin for two cartons of Chesterfields.

Once we struck the deal, an officer came with me to the Nabob, bringing with him the cigarettes and taking back a bottle of gin. Unfortunately, our relationship with the Houston was short-lived; they were off to the Far East later that night.

By this time, we no longer were just an Avenger-only ship; we'd been joined by four (sometimes five) Wildcat fighter aircraft and their pilots, mostly New Zealanders. Their purpose was to serve primarily as fleet protection or to detect submarines lying on the surface recharging their batteries. At once, I thought these pilots should have the new Frank anti-G suits, so I arranged for five of them to be sent up from the Naval Air Station at Eastleigh. Much to my surprise, Jim Long, the technician in charge, flew up the very next day, bringing with him five of the suits. Jim and I had become good friends at the Naval Air Station and, as it now seemed we were going to be in Belfast longer than previously expected, he suggested that if some of the suits didn't fit that would be a good reason for me to come down to Eastleigh to get ones that did fit and incidentally, have a little visit. As these suits were top secret, they had to be transported either by air or under armed guard. As the latter was not feasible, I asked the captain to allow me to fly to Eastleigh to get them. He agreed. I asked one of the pilots that I'd gotten to know well, New Zealander Angus Watson, if he'd like to make the flight to Eastleigh. He agreed, and we set about making our plans to leave the next day. Then Bobby heard about it and decided he and his observer, Parky Parkinson, would take all of us in his plane. Of course, that changed everything.

When we took off the next day the flight plan, as I understood it, was that we were to fly in visual contact (with the ground) and under two thousand feet. Bobby followed this plan for less than ten minutes; by then we were above the clouds and we stayed there. After flying for an hour and a half or so, I asked Parky where we were. His answer was, "I've no idea. But don't worry, we'll be there soon."

After maybe another half hour, we made a sharp descent and broke clouds, and below us I saw we were coming in over what looked to me the edge of a very busy harbour, protected by a breakwater. Then I saw this was no ordinary breakwater, but one that included that Phoenix caisson I'd seen in Southampton and a very large number of sunken ships. I knew instantly this had to be one of the Mulberrys (artificial harbours) that I'd recently heard the British had built and that this one must be the one at Arromanches, Normandy. Protected from the open sea by the Mulberry, several large ships discharged their cargoes onto trucks on pier-heads, which were connected to the shore by floating roadways. Smaller craft dashed around the harbour. On land, trucks seemed to be unloading their cargoes, and piles of what looked like ammunition and other supplies stood all around. Several roads led inland. Off shore, a number of warships were anchored. I knew this was an extremely unhealthy place for us to be, for the Navy didn't like any aircraft flying over them, even if we did have invasion stripes on our wings. Of course, Bobby knew this too, and immediately I heard our engine rev's increase and felt the higher G's as our tight turn pressed me hard into my seat. We were out of there and I took a deep breath. It was marvelous to have had this glimpse of the real war!

Before long we were landing, to my disappointment, not at East-leigh as I had expected, but at the nearby Royal Naval Air Station at Lee-on-Solent. Then Bobby disappeared. We didn't know where, but we all knew there must be a woman waiting not far away. My plans for a day or two get together with my friends in Eastleigh disappeared.

The next two days showed no sign of Bobby. We sent signals back to the Nabob, not twice, stating that our return was delayed by weather. On the third day, Angus, Parky, and I flew over to nearby RNAS Eastleigh to pick up our anti-G suits and to briefly visit our friends there. This was not at all what I'd hoped. I was able to see Irene for only a few minutes, with no chance for a real talk or to explain to her why I had been such a dolt when I was with her a few weeks back when I was on leave.

The fourth day, Bobby finally returned, and we started for home. It turned out that our journey was not without peril. Bobby had decided that the shortest way to the Nabob would be to fly not over, but through Wales. At first this was fine, flying through one beautiful verdant valley after another. But suddenly, we all saw that this new valley had an abrupt end. Bobby made what must have been at least a rate four turn. We were so close to the trees that, had I had my hand outside the plane, I could have picked leaves off the trees. After that it was up and over and around Wales leaving the valleys of Wales far below. By this time, the Nabob was comfortably in the Western Approaches, about one hundred miles west of Ireland. We landed without further ado.

The next morning at Sick Call, one of our crew was complaining of abdominal pain and vomiting. He said it had started about 2200 the previous evening, but thought it would get better so he didn't do anything about it until he came to sick call. I examined him. He had a little fever and right lower quadrant abdominal tenderness. By this time his disease had progressed to the extent that when he walked, he bent forward and to the right side, a classical sign of appendicitis. A rectal exam confirmed that diagnosis. I called Walter and he agreed.

Then we had to decide what to do. We could have put him in a plane and flown him to a shore hospital, but that would delay any treatment for several hours and we had a perfectly good operating set-up at hand; moreover, we were anxious to use it. We considered the situation and decided we'd operate. PO Hines and the other tiffies began to ready the operating room. Walter and I read our surgical manual to refresh our memories about how to do the procedure, for I was the last one to have done an appendectomy, and that was about a year ago. We enlisted our dentist, George Craig, an Army captain, who had joined us in New York, as a back-up anesthetist. We sent word to Captain Lay that we were going to operate and would like him to keep the ship as steady as possible for the duration of the procedure.

At last, all was ready. I started an intravenous drip, and then Walter used it as a route to inject Pentothal. Even before the count of ten, the patient was anesthetized. Then we shifted over to a closed-ether technique and Craig took charge of that, under our supervision. Walter was the chief surgeon, and I was his assistant. Carter was the scrub nurse, and the other tiffies doing whatever odd jobs came along, with Hines supervising everything. From the beginning, all went well. Walter opened the abdomen and quickly isolated the appendix. It had slightly perforated, but we were able to remove it without difficulty. We had reviewed all the steps to this point, but had not read some important details about closing. Then we realized that both of us had forgotten some technical details, including what kind of gut to use in closing the peritoneum and whether it was continuous or interrupted stitching. We also faced the same problems for the muscle layer. Walter and I discussed these problems; sometimes I was pretty sure of what to do, and I'd take over and do it, sometimes he would.

We finished the operation in about an hour, and would have done so sooner had we not been slowed down by these discussions. Finally, I placed a Miller-Abbott gastric tube that had a little rubber balloon at its tip and blew it up slightly to keep it from coming out. As soon as we finished, Walter made an ingenious device, using three inter-changeable empty vaco-liter bottles and attached it to the gastric tube. This allowed continuous suction of the stomach contents. It worked fabulously. The intravenous solution that I'd started before the operation began was now changed to five percent glucose. This completed the post-operative procedures. We all felt very satisfied with what we'd done and notified the captain that we had successfully finished. He did not reply.

About three the next morning, SBA Henri Lebrun aroused me from a deep sleep by saying, "Doctor Read, something is happening to our patient. Come quickly."

I jumped out of my bed and ran to our hospital ward. Our patient was lying on his back in the Gatch hospital bed I was so proud of, holding the gastric tube with both hands. "It's going down," he said, an anxious look on his face. I was delighted. I knew that it meant his intestinal motility had already become active and that the intestinal muscles were pulling the balloon and so the tube downwards. It was a very positive sign. I deflated the balloon and withdrew the gastric tube. The remainder of his post-operative course was routine. We discharged him and sent him on leave five days later.

Both Walter and I thought that this successful operation would be a great positive for us insofar as establishing in the crew some confidence in our competence. I believed it did, but maybe that was just wishful thinking.

Only a day or two later, I was standing in the starboard catwalk beside the flight deck talking to one of my tiffies when I noticed how the petty officer in charge of moving aircraft around the deck was directing his deck crew as they pushed an Avenger up the deck toward the bow. He was supposed to do this by standing facing his crew and the plane and beckoning them with both hands to bring the aircraft towards him. At intervals he was supposed to stop, clench his hands, the signal to stop pushing the plane, turn, walk forward to a new position, turn and again motion his crew to push the aircraft toward him. But he did not do it this time. Instead, he was walking slowly backward while simultaneously beckoning his crew to keep on pushing the aircraft forward. All of us knew the forward elevator was down. Surely, he knew that too and that he would stop. But no, he kept on moving backwards until, with one last backward step, he disappeared into the elevator space. I raced down to the hangar deck, fearing the worst. But he was lucky. He'd landed on his back on the wing of a parked Avenger and had only a few bruises and a simple forearm fracture.

One of the pleasures that we enjoyed many times when we were anchored in the Clyde off Gourock was waking up in the morning and seeing the Queen Mary anchored nearby. During the next few days, she would be surrounded with activity, as first the fifteen thousand troops they had on board disembarked, followed by various kinds of cargo, and after being refueled, embarked those lucky enough to be returning to the United States. Then, as mysteriously as she had arrived, one morning she was gone, only to have the Queen Elizabeth soon appear and go through the same procedures.

When we stayed overnight off Bangor on the south side of Belfast Lough, golf was now almost always the order of the evening for the captain and some of his officer friends, unless the weather was unpleasant. Being a tennis player rather than a golfer, I failed to understand the depth of the fervor for golf that these players had for the game. Most of us, both officers and men, went ashore these nights, attending such delights as a large and beautiful cinema, complete with a sunken organ that rose with its music playing from below to entertain the movie goers between shows. On one occasion, one of our crew was sitting in the back row, smoking (allowed), and apparently getting intimate with a woman he'd met. Unfortunately for him, when she finished her cigarette she chose to butt it on his bared penis. Back on board the Nabob, we did our best to help him cope with his pain.

Our daytime flying activities continued: Navexes (navigation exercises), anti-submarine exercises and many others; the purpose of which I had no knowledge. I concentrated on my sick bay duties and being sure I was always present beside the flight deck for all landings and take-offs. I never found them routine. These pilots were landing Avengers, the largest single engine aircraft in the world, not only on a small moving target, but also one that was continually rising and falling several feet, with a space available for landing of no more than three hundred and fifty feet in length and less than eighty feet in width. This was a task that required an unusual level of skill, especially at night on a blacked-out ship. I was more than aware of the risks involved.

For example, on 14 July, Bobby Bradshaw broke his hook when landing and ran into the barrier, damaging his propeller and engine. Then, on both 21 and 22 July, Don Cash had hook problems, the first time causing him to crash into the barrier, and the second time doing enough damage to his plane that it had to be replaced.

The next morning, we learned that a tame aircraft would be coming out from shore pulling a drogue (a funnel-shaped device) for gunnery practice. It arrived promptly and made a pass down the port side of the ship from bow to stern. All the Oerlikons on that side fired at the drogue. Making a port turn, it then flew up the starboard side, the Oerlikons on that side having a go at the target. Crossing our bow and climbing to a higher altitude, he began another pass on the port side. This time it was the Bofors guns turn. About halfway through his pass, the puffs from the explosion of the shells appeared, not behind the aircraft, but in front. Abruptly, the aircraft turned away. A few minutes later it returned, no drogue in sight. The pilot signaled, "Please note I was pulling the drogue, not pushing it."

This aircraft never did return. I had no difficulty understanding why this pilot didn't want to be a target another time. I wouldn't have either. But I enjoyed the way he told us that he was finished.

Apart from that mistake, other problems also occurred during this exercise. Some of the Oerlikons that were converted from single to twin mountings in the recent Liverpool refit overloaded their circuits and shorted out and so lost the use of the Mark IV automatic gun sights. A revision of these alterations soon followed. The two 5-inch guns mounted on our stern fired once. The noise was deafening and the vibrations so severe that everything not tied down fell to the deck. We all hoped that they would never be fired again. All in all, it was not a very successful day, but at least we found out these problems so we could correct them.

A day or two later, Don Cash flew over to the HMS Charger to collect the Flag Officer Carrier Trainer and his staff. Don made a perfect landing when he returned, taxied forward and stopped at the bridge. There the captain, the flight commander and Bobby (in full uniform), as well as onlookers, waited. Much to everyone's amusement, the admiral, attempting to exit the plane with his rather large posterior first, got stuck in the door. All of us watched as he tried first to get out and then to get back into the aircraft. His actions were really quite funny, and it was with some difficulty that none of us laughed outright. However, after a lot of tugging and pulling, he finally reversed his position and managed to get out, one leg at a time.

A day or two after that, on the evening of 28 July, I happened to overhear the conversation, not a quiet one, between Bobby Bradshaw, the Flight Commander, Lieutenant Commander Sidney-Turner, and Captain Lay. The flight commander was a passed over two and a half striper and was known to be very anxious to get the third stripe that, of course, would give him naval tenure. For that reason, we all thought he was a 'yes-man' to the captain, rather than being primarily interested in the welfare of the squadron members. What I heard of in this conversation was that Captain Lay seemed determined to have an anti-submarine exercise that night, even though we were in the Irish Sea, where submarines were most unusual. The weather had been bad all day and still was that evening. Bobby showed the captain that there were ten-tenths clouds at five hundred feet, with rain and patches of sea fog. Flying would be justifiable if there was a serious impending danger, but to do it just as an exercise was nothing but a risk to our pilots. Bobby did not believe anyone should fly. Lay insisted there was a submarine risk and, as usual, the flight commander supported him. Because of this supposed submarine menace, the crews would carry armed depth charges.

In accordance with the usual rule for anti-submarine night flying, only one aircraft at a time catapulted into the night sky. I was always worried about anyone landing on this blacked-out ship at night where the only lights, one set on either side of the ship, were slanted so that they could only be seen from above and astern. At the appointed time, Don Cash, who had already previously completed two-night anti-submarine fights and was probably the most skillful and experienced pilot in the squadron, took off. About the time of his scheduled return, some two hours later, I went to my usual spot by the first wire, where a cold, swirling wind pelted my face with rain. It wasn't long before an aircraft emerged from the darkness, quickly disappeared in a patch of sea fog, only to reappear, but too late to attempt a landing. Gavin waved his wands, signaling the plane go around again. I watched as the plane flew by on the port side as it was supposed to do. I noted it was F for Freddy, Don Cash's plane. To get out of the rain and the cold, I walked forward to the ready room, prepared to wait until Don came around again. But just as I entered the ready room, there came the unmistakable sounds of not one, but two depth charges exploding. Immediately we all feared the worst, because we all knew Don and his crew was carrying two 300-pound depth charges, set to explode at twenty-five feet.

I was still in the Ready Room, numbed by the disaster that had just unfolded, and especially the loss of the pilot to whom I felt closest, when I heard my page; I was to report to the starboard entrance pod at once. I didn't know why I was paged, but I got there as quickly as I could. There someone announced that our accompanying destroyer plane-guard had sighted Don floating in the water in his K-dinghy. They'd picked him up and were bringing him to us on one of their boats.

I didn't need to hear the rest. A one-person ladder led from the sponson down some twenty feet to a platform at the water line that measured about three feet by six feet. I descended the ladder as quickly as I could. The ship's boat was just coming along side. As they closed, all the rowers on the near side of the lifeboat simultaneously lifted their oars to a vertical position, allowing it to come along side. Don, obviously unconscious, had been draped over the nearside gunnels. The boat was rising and falling with each wave. At the trough of the wave, the boat was about three feet below my feet, at its crest the water was just about half way to my knees. I quickly realized I would have to grab him as he passed by. The next time the boat rose, I somehow managed to get hold of the unconscious Don at his waist and hung on to him as the boat was falling. Then I got him in a fireman's lift, something I'd heard described, but had never done before. Somehow, I carried him up the twenty feet to the top of the ladder. He didn't even feel heavy. There, four others took over, put him on a stretcher and carried him down to our operating room. I followed.

When I got there a few minutes later, Don had regained con-sciousness. Both Walter and I examined him. We found no evidence of broken bones or internal injuries, only lacerations on his forehead and around his nose. When I saw the injuries, I asked Walter if I could do the surgery because working with Dr. Happy Baxter during my surgical internship, he'd shown me exactly how to repair such a laceration. Walter agreed and stood by, cheering me on. I wanted fine steel wire, but having none, I used the finest silk suturing thread we had. I avoided using a local anesthetic to avoid any distortion of the tissues. It took time and a lot of small stitches, but subsequently I was satisfied with what I had done.

A little while after I finished, I asked Don what happened.

He'd come out of patch of fog too late to risk a landing with the depth charges he'd been carrying, got a wave-off, and so flew off down the port side, as he was supposed to do. Then he'd made a mistake. Instead of watching his instruments, he'd looked back at the ship. That was not the thing to do because he'd lost track of his attitude. He should have been looking at his instruments. Hitting the water had been a complete surprise. Water started coming in over the cowling and he couldn't get out because he was jammed back by the engine. The next thing he knew, he was floating in the K dinghy. Then he'd been picked up by the guys in the boat, though he didn't know how they'd found him.

I was surprised that he remembered that much, considering the undoubted severity of his concussion.

Unfortunately, despite a five-hour search, we never found Cash's observer Wheeler, a remarkable cartoonist, or his tail gunner Bissett.

The next morning, Walter accompanied Don when he went by ambulance to the naval hospital near Greenoch. There, Walter said, a said-to-be famous plastic surgeon had made complimentary remarks about my plastic surgery; saying nothing more needed to be done.

The Nabob was then anchored in the Clyde off Gouroch, with a sailing time of 1500 hours. As Walter arrived at the quay side to take our ship's boat back, he saw the Nabob leave its mooring. It was ten minutes before the appointed hour. Walter got in the boat he had come in and with the bos'n driving it at high speed, caught up to the Nabob.

Walter then climbed up the same ladder I'd used the night before. Just as he reached his cabin, a messenger arrived requesting his immediate presence in the captain's cabin. Walter, whose relation-ships with the captain had not been good, was annoyed but, of course, complied. I went with him. The captain wasted no time. "You were late arriving on board. I'm going to have you court martialed for that."

Walter was livid, and snapped back that he would have the captain court-martialed for leaving ten minutes ahead of the scheduled time.

At this point I left, but I learned later that nothing more happened, so they must have called it a draw. But there was no question in my mind that Walter did not like or respect Captain Lay and that it was probably mutual.

The next afternoon I was watching for our four Wildcats (F4F's) who were due to return from some anti-submarine exercises, so I was not surprised when I heard the command from the loudspeakers on the bride bridge, "Stand by to receive four Wildcats."

I hadn't gotten to know their pilots very well in the short time they'd been with us. They were younger and more volatile than the other pilots and flew their planes more vigorously. Most of them were Kiwis. The first three landed without problems. But the last one wasn't coming in on the mid-line of the deck, having drifted off toward the starboard side, heading straight for me. Watching the plane approach, I prepared to protect myself as best I could by getting partially under the cover of the over-hanging flight deck. The pilot did correct quite a lot, so I didn't feel like I was in real danger, but he was still far too close to the starboard edge for comfort. I kept watching. Finally, his right wheel touched down, only about three or less feet from the edge of the deck, right in front of me. The extreme tension on the arrestor wire then yanked the plane sharply back towards the center. As this was happening, the three-quarter inch diameter arrestor wire pulled out of its receptor (the wire did not break, as reported) and began to rapidly slither across the deck, aiming directly for Gavin Waite, our batsman. I climbed up on the deck and began to run across to him, horrified by the thought of what might happen to Gavin, fearing I might find him in two pieces. I saw the wire strike him on the forehead as he was falling backwards into his safety net. I found him in one piece but unconscious, both his face and forehead badly damaged. I administered first aid. Walter and several of the tiffies soon joined me, and together, we carried him down to the Sick Bay.

Gavin spent the next six months in the same hospital in Greenwich where Don Cash had been admitted. The surgeries that Gavin had to undergo, Don later said, made the surgery I'd done on him seem minor.

Chapter Fourteen

A Loaf of White Bread

The next day Admiral Lyster, the Flag Officer Carrier Training, arrived to inspect us. Apparently we passed, but more importantly, we learned we were no longer attached to the Commander-in-Chief of Western Approaches. Instead, we now were to join the First Cruiser Squadron of the Royal Navy at Scapa Flow. I thought this to be strange. After all this time during which we'd been practicing anti-submarine warfare, we were now going to join the Royal Navy Home Fleet. I began to wonder if the Royal Navy had decided on some special plan; one in which they were going to use our squadron as a sacrificial lamb, just as the British had used one brigade of the Canadian 2nd Division in the stupidly planned and disastrous attack on Dieppe, and the many times I'd read about in the history of the First World War when they used Canadians in a similar fashion. For the first time, I realized that we were not what I'd call a real Canadian ship, but only a Canadian-manned Royal Navy aircraft carrier, so the situation wasn't quite comparable. I felt both let down and greatly concerned. What did the Royal Navy have in mind for us?

The next day, I learned that Lieutenant Commander Sidney-Turner had been relieved of his position of Commander-Flying. We assumed this was because he had not protected the squadron from the captain, resulting in Don Cash's crash and the loss of his crew. Both Walter and I thought it also meant that the Admiralty had decided that Captain Lay was not justified in insisting on the flight that night.

I saw nothing for me to do as Sidney-Turner left the ship. Obviously knowing his naval career was over, he looked very depressed. In spite of everything, I felt sorry for him. A few weeks later we heard he'd committed suicide. His replacement, Lieutenant Commander (A)

R. J. H. Stephenson, I never got to know, but he looked like a person capable of standing up to the captain.

Gavin Waite's replacement was Lieutenant (A) Rose, DSO, one of only five survivors of Squadron 825. In 1942, that squadron had made a suicidal attack on the German battleships Scharnhorst and Gneisenau as they were escaping up the English Channel. I did look forward to getting to know him.

With all of this coming and going, it seemed like a good time for me to go to Edinburgh to replenish out liquor supply. Apparently Seagrams VO Whiskey, Captain Lay's favorite, all of the four hundred cases of which he had ordered in Vancouver, was now in short supply. I assumed that he must have done a great deal of entertaining.

First, I got a list of the Spirit Houses in Edinburgh, but when I walked into the offices of the first on my list, Cadenhead's Whisky Shop and saw all the myriads of bottles available, I became keenly aware of my lack of knowledge of all kinds of whiskey. It took but a moment for the gentleman who waited on me to realize that. He insisted that Scotch was the only true whisky. Those could be single malts or blends with different amounts of other whiskies or even neutral grain spirits. After those, there were VO rye whiskeys or corn-based Bourbons, among others. Then he poured small amounts of seven Scotch whiskeys and rye (VO) whiskey in a series of small glasses. I drank, I think, all seven of his samples, one after another, with pauses in between. Each seemed to taste a little different. But not being much of a drinker, even this small amount of liquor had a noticeable effect, so I was not exactly sure what, or how much I'd ordered. I asked about payment. He seemed in no hurry at all about that, simply asking me a few questions and said that's all he needed to know.

I inquired about delivery.

They couldn't take it to my ship, but he suggested that I fly it on. They could have the shipment to the naval air station in Donnibristle, just across the Firth of Forth, in two days.

Afterwards I walked slowly the length of Princes Street, recovering from my whisky tasting, window shopping and gazing up at Edinburgh Castle. Finally, I took a cab to visit my Montreal patient's family, the Wallaces, at 102 Ravelstone Dykes. I'd brought with me a loaf of white bread and a pound of butter, items I'd heard that had been very scarce almost since the war began five years ago. I knocked, the door opened, a fine-looking middle-aged gentleman appeared. I introduced myself and told him that I had looked after their daughter, Marjorie, in Montreal. He seemed to know about that and invited me in.

I was almost embarrassed by the way they treated my little gifts as if they were manna. They hadn't seen white bread for four years and couldn't remember when they last saw butter. They insisted I stay for dinner. I did and that was embarrassing, for they were having a tiny roast of beef, probably their week's ration, and they insisted I have some and not just a tiny piece.

During the course of the evening, Mr. Wallace told me how busy they were, planning for the month-long Festival they were going to have every August in Edinburgh, beginning as soon as possible after the war was over. They planned to include a variety of concerts in the park and other events as well. They were even going to have buskers on the Golden Mile. He seemed very sure the war would soon be over and that it was important to plan now for the future of the Festival.

It had been a most enjoyable evening, but the time came when I really had to leave to get the 2300 train back to Glasgow and so on to Gouroch. But when I got to Waverly Station, I realized I should have left much earlier, because there was a long queue that stretched the entire length of the station. I soon found out that 1 August had been Glasgow's civic holiday, so seemingly everybody in Glasgow had come to Edinburgh where there'd been no bomb damage and one could find everything. I walked past these tired shoppers, feeling very embarrassed by using my naval officer's uniform in this way, but I felt it was more important for me to get to Glasgow and onward than it was for these shoppers. When I reached the gate, I felt I was brazen when I asked the gatekeeper to allow me to go through to the platform, where London to Glasgow via Edinburgh train was to arrive. I was both surprised and embarrassed when he let me through. I was the first person on the platform, but I made the unthinking mistake of standing at the back of platform.

When the train came in, the gate opened, and the waiting shoppers descended. I suddenly found myself about as far from a door of the train as was possible. Consequently, even by pushing and shoving, I was barely able to get on board. Clearly, I was going to have to stand the whole trip to Glasgow. Fortunately, everyone seemed to be in a good mood and it was easy to strike up conversations, especially as the young woman standing within inches of me was very attractive. She introduced herself as Jennifer. When I told her I was hoping to go through to Gourock that night, she told me that I hadn't a chance. This train was so late that we'd never get to Glasgow in time for me to catch that train. The older woman standing beside her, who turned out to be her mother, agreed, and they insisted that I spend the night at their place. She had two other daughters with her, both younger than Jennifer.

When we arrived in Glasgow, off we went together. I walked with Jennifer, the others trailing along behind. Their home was very comfortable, not too far from the station and soon everyone except Jennifer and I had gone to bed. We visited over a cup of tea and then called it a night. In the morning, I awoke as she came into my room and gave me a quick, impersonal kiss. After I remembered where I was, we visited for a few minutes. Then she left, taking with her, much to my surprise, my trousers and my shoes. I wondered what she was going to do with them; I went back to sleep. Sometime later she again awakened me by coming in with my trousers, freshly pressed, and shoes, newly shined. She then left, saying my breakfast was ready and that she had to go to work. After dressing, I joined her mother who had prepared an elegant breakfast for me that even included kippered herrings, a favorite of mine. This, I thought, was even better than Nova Scotian hospitality.

Two days later, on 3 August, I stood at the end of the runway at RNAS Merlin in Donnibristle while the whisky and the VO I'd ordered was loaded on one of our Avengers. It filled all the space that could be used for cargo. When the loading was completed, I checked the cargo and the plane flew off to the Nabob. The interesting thing about this airstrip was that at the end of the runway, a 550-foot volcanic rock prevented the left turn that pilots usually make on take-off. Instead here they had to turn to the right. I think everybody, including even the airport's dog, reminded the pilot about that. Even so, I was relieved when I saw the plane flying in the sky above and beyond this unusual hazard.

The Spirit House had a car waiting for me and I was soon off for Gouroch and the Nabob.

Chapter Fifteen

A Long, but Good, Day

At last, after more than six weeks of these work-ups in the Irish Sea, the HMS Nabob, the first Canadian-manned aircraft carrier, was ready for action. It had been a frustrating, seemingly unending process, the long, long refit, followed by weeks punctuated by engine breakdowns, lousy weather making flying impossible, minor crashes and, at the end, the loss of Don and the death of his crew, and finally by Gavin's serious accident. It had seemed like it had just been one damned thing after the other. Sometimes I even wondered if with all the things that had gone wrong was the Nabob really snake-bit, as was raised as a question back during the Vancouver days. Then I remembered that she was 77, and with that lucky number, she would survive whatever might happen to her.

But now as we slipped our anchorage off Gouroch and headed north up the west coast of Scotland, protected by the islands of the Outer Hebrides, our morale was high. I was sure everyone on board was excited to finally be joining the action. This was not what we'd expected, but at least it was to be action of some type. But again, I began to wonder if there wasn't some special reason why we were about to become a part of the Royal Navy's Home Fleet.

The next afternoon, when we entered Scapa Flow, the home of the British Home Fleet in the Orkney Islands, our band, borrowed from the building Canadian cruiser, Ontario, proudly played *O Canada, Roll Along Wavy Navy, Roll Along,* and *The Maple Leaf Forever.* Standing on the flight deck, we applauded and yelled, "Yeah, Nabob! Yeah, Canada!" We were a relaxed, happy crew, looking forward to some real action.

A signal from Rear Admiral R.R. McGrigor, the Flag Officer of the first Cruiser Squadron, soon informed us that we were now a member of the Royal Navy's Force 4, attached to the HMS Indefatigeable, a fleet aircraft carrier, and under his command. We also learned that the other ships in Force 4 were the HMS Trumpeter, a sister carrier identical to the Nabob, and eight destroyers, including two Canadians, the Algonquin and the Sioux, although I didn't know about them being with us until later. To us on the Nabob, and to me in particular, the important thing was that, at long last we had joined the fight against Hitler's Nazi Germany for which I had been readying myself since September 1939.

The very next day we learned the plan of our first operation was called Offspring. Our Avengers, and those from the Trumpeter, were to lay mines in the inland passage of Norway between Alesund and Kristiansund. This was to force enemy shipping from the safe channel provided by the coastal islands and fjords of the coast out to the open sea to become targets for Allied aircraft and our waiting submarines. In preparation, another Avenger (presumably a spare) and two more Wildcats were added to our squadron's inventory.

On 9 August we sailed, and two days later reached the operational area. Standing in my usual position on the starboard catwalk near the first arrestor wire, I watched when at precisely 1300, two of our Wildcats took off into a cloudy sky. They were to provide fleet protection.

The twelve Avengers of our squadron took off, followed by the twelve Avengers of Squadron 856 from the Trumpeter. Then Fireflies, Seafires, and Hellcats from the Indefatigable followed to provide protection for the two attacking squadrons. They all headed northeast, their targets the Channel Islands of Lepsorey and Haarhamsfjord of Norway.

The mines they were to drop by parachute were called Smart Mines and were programmed to lie dormant on the bottom where they couldn't be swept. Then, at various intervals during the next thirty days, each mine in turn would become activated. Then, the acoustic signals of the propeller of a passing ship would turn on one of the mine's propulsion apparatus and that mine would be primed to attack.

At 1530, both the Nabob and the Trumpeter turned into the wind, a clear indication that our aircraft would soon be landing, as staying on a straight course was dangerous in these submarine-infested waters. I began searching the northeast sky in hopes of seeing our returning planes, but it was a long anxiety-filled ten minutes before I saw them. I began counting as soon as they entered the landing circuit. I got to twelve and, to my relief, saw no signs of damage. One by one they landed. As usual, it was easy for me to recognize two of them by the way they landed. Keith Stevens, sitting on a pillow to help him see straight ahead, made his usual very tight turn, straightening out just before he came over the round end of our ship. Bill Black came straight in from way back.

I was jubilant when I joined the aircrew in the Ready Room, but I was surprised that they didn't seem more excited. Maybe, I thought, perhaps that was because they had another flight to make as soon as their planes were refueled and re-armed and they'd had a bite to eat. I asked Bill Reeks, an observer, about how he felt.

He replied that they had been a complete surprise, so there wasn't any opposition. It was just like all the practice attacks they'd made on similar sites in northwest Scotland, and they'd done many of them. They dropped our mines and they shot up a number of Messerschmitts 110's on the ground, set a barracks on fire, and sank a minesweeper. It was pretty satisfying all right, but that was not too much to get excited about. At least, Reeks rationalized, they were going back again in a little while. The enemy would probably be waiting for them.

And they were. Our squadrons took two hours and thirty minutes to make the round trip, ten minutes longer than the first time, but the Nabob squadron escaped without loss. The Trumpeter lost one Avenger; the Indefatigable lost a Firefly and two Seafires. By 2045, our aircrews were quietly celebrating. After eleven months of training, they said that at long last they'd gotten their grips on the war.

Then I noticed that Eric Roberts, one of the pilots, was sitting quietly by himself. This was most unusual, for Eric was an enthusiastic and active young man, not ordinarily given to quiet introspection. I walked over to him and sat down beside him. As he seemed a little down, I asked if he wanted to talk.

He told me that he'd had an odd experience during the second attack. The first attack had gone well, but on their second, the Germans were ready for them, and Eric had soon realized that this time it wasn't just another exercise. After they'd dropped the mine, he'd flown around looking for whatever he could find to shoot up. He found a medium-size craft, maybe a dredge. It looked like an interesting target and he told his crew what he was going to do and began the attack. He'd just gotten nicely into it when something within told him, no, don't do it. So he changed his mind and turned away. Seconds later, an Avenger from the Trumpeter flew by and began his attack on the same target. When he looked again, it was just in time to see him crash into the sea.

Putting my arm around his shoulder, I gave him a hug and sat with him for a long while, not saying much. It had been a long, but a good day.

Two days of almost hurricane force gales featured the first part of our trip back from Norway, which the Nabob mastered despite much active rolling and pitching, spray even reaching the flight deck as she plowed into each towering wave. As usual on days like this, there were many empty seats at the dining tables.

The next afternoon I visited the radar plot cabin. A large Plexiglas screen on which there were a series of concentric circles stood on one side of the room. My bunkmate Schoolie, who also functioned as a radar officer, explained to me that the center of the screen was our position and the area covered was the airspace between the coast of Scotland and Norway.

It happened that very soon after I arrived there a blip showed up on the screen headed away from the coast of Norway. The room became very quiet.

"That's a bandit," Schoolie said, his voice betraying excitement.

I wanted to know why he was so very certain.

It turned out that all of our aircraft carried a Friend or Foe Indicator (IFF) that showed up on the radar screen. They were changed at least every day, sometimes more frequently.

Scant minutes later, a blip showing the IFF of the day emerged from the coast of Scotland and headed toward the bandit. Soon the bandit changed its course. Almost immediately, our friendly blip was vectored directly toward the enemy. Changes like these happened several times. Overall, our blip seemed to move faster than theirs. During the next twenty minutes or so, the two blips became closer and closer, until finally, they merged. I crossed my fingers. One or two of the others bit their fingernails. Everyone looked tense.

Then there was only one blip. It was not only showing our IFF, but it was heading back toward Scotland. I was relieved, and I could feel my whole body begin to relax.

Then I realized I was exhausted. It seemed to be the way with the others too; everyone was quiet, not a single one of the half dozen persons present either had clapped or cheered. Everyone was still, quiet; no one spoke. Some sat leaning forward on their chairs with their head in their hands, others leaned back with their legs out stretched, others just stood as if transfixed. In a while we dispersed silently. It had been an intensely emotional experience. I thought about how it was such an abstract way to fight a war; two blips on a screen. Of course, this would be old hat for all those who had been involved in the Battle of Britain.

Later on that day we found out we weren't immediately returning to Scapa Flow, but to Rosyth, a Royal Navy base on the Firth of Forth not far, but on the opposite shore from Edinburgh. Rumors soon said that we were going there to pick up special big mines. When I heard this, I wondered whether they were special big mines for our next operation. Obviously, this first operation had been just a warm-up for something much bigger. I pondered what it would be. Anyway, for now, it meant we were going to have a few hours of shore leave in Edinburgh tomorrow afternoon and evening until 2100. That would be the time when the last train to Rosyth left.

When I emerged from Waverly station, my pace was leisurely as I walked down a sun-warmed Princess Street, again window shopping and enjoying the view of the flower-graced park and Edinburgh Castle, a spectacular scene. This city had escaped any bombing, so the other pedestrians, including many from the three services, most of who were probably on leave, seemed more relaxed than in Glasgow or Liverpool. This time I had two loaves of white bread and two pounds of butter for the Wallaces. It was more than I had the first time, when my single loaf of bread and the pound of butter had looked so small on their table. Again, they welcomed my gifts as if they were precious jewels and again insisted I stay for dinner. However, this time I had the excuse that I had leave to join our aircrew for a celebration at the Aperitif Restaurant on Frederick Street. There everyone was in high spirits, so, led by some of our Kiwis, we did a Haka, the Maori war dance, complete with its sounds, much foot stamping and sticking out of tongues. The manager immediately threatened to close the bar. Our response: if he did, we'd repeat the Haka. The bar stayed open. But I spent the last hour before the train departed, sitting on a park bench talking to a delightful Scottish school teacher from Dollar that I'd met at the restaurant. She said she was on a summer break.

In the darkness of the blacked-out train on my way back to the Nabob, I thought over the events of the past few days. It seemed to me that our first action was like playing an exhibition game against an unrated team at the beginning of the fall football season. We'd won that game without much difficulty, but with the season now starting, bigger challenges lay ahead. How tough would the next game be?

We sailed from Rosyth at midnight. As we approached one of the gate ships controlling the anti-submarine nets that guarded the Firth of Forth, it became evident that the Nabob was not lined up properly. When the danger of collision became evident, Captain Lay first ordered a twenty and then a thirty-degree alteration in course. This caused the Nabob's stern to swing around so that our protruding aerials knocked the mast off of the southernmost gate-ship, the HMS Bishopgate. Falling on one of our starboard sponsons, the mast destroyed one of our Oerlikon machine guns. So close were we to the gate-ship, the same sponson damaged the gate ship's port lifeboat supports.

Our squadron's Line Book recorded the episode:

> On reaching the harbour boom there was a loud crash, followed by a report from the starboard forward lookout, 'Unidentified mast lying on deck, Sir' upon which——on the bridge gave 'thirty (degrees) to port,' thus striking the unseen enemy another crushing blow with the stern of our vessel. A further report came from the after lookout 'Unidentified commissioning pennant and two objects appearing to be a pair of black balls on the starboard after sponson, Sir.' Having by all this commotion given away our presence, we made off immediately at high speed. The success of the action is borne out by the last report from the after lookout, 'Ship astern flashing franticly to send tug immediately. Light appears to be very close to water.'

The Line Book continued: "Dawn found the Nabob safely many miles out to sea. The radar department refuses to admit their share in the success of the operation, but of course, this is merely their usual modesty."

By breakfast time we were back in Scapa Flow. By then someone had posted on the bulletin board in our wardroom: "The Admiralty announced that last night HMS Nabob was in action with one of the gate ships on the Firth of Forth. From this action, one of our Oerlikons failed to return."

Later, when I came on deck, I saw that there were many more warships at anchor in Scapa Flow now than there had been when we'd set out last week. I counted at least four battleships, five fleet carriers, a squadron of heavy cruisers and twenty or more destroyers. I couldn't imagine that the Royal Navy would assemble as powerful Home Fleet as this without a good reason. Something big was in the wind.

Chapter Sixteen

Always Walking

I was excited that we might finally be involved in a major operation. This, I knew, was what we'd all been working toward—making a major contribution to the fight against Nazism. We were ready. We were willing. We were capable. We'd worked hard and completed those weeks of work-ups in the Irish Sea, and we'd done well in our first operation, small as it had been. Our ship's crew was young and inexperienced, many never even having been to sea before, but I'd seen they were hardworking, co-operative, and intelligent. They'd learned their roles quickly. Our group of tiffies had already proven themselves to be well-trained, reliable, and competent. Certainly, the flight deck crew, a group of six footers, could move those big Avengers around the deck with seemingly little effort. Our squadron, Royal Navy Fleet Air Arm Squadron 852, had just demonstrated they had the high skills, morale, and preparation for whatever lay ahead. Furthermore, they had a leader already proven that he was extraordinary.

The very next day, after I finished attending to those that came to Sick Call, I talked for a longer time than usual with Walter. By this point we had become close friends, and I had come to know he was an exemplary physician. I'd seen him cope with some difficult situations, especially when standing up to the captain, who was often mean-spirited and self-centered. Although it hadn't seemed to have been a problem for Walter, it certainly must not have been pleasant. I felt very fortunate to have him as both my superior officer and my friend.

I asked him what he thought our next operation might be. The ever-present twinkle in his eye disappeared and he was quiet for a time, as if he were considering my question. He didn't know, of course, but with all the power we could see around us, it must have been pretty important. Walter suspected that it would be the German battleship known as the Tirpitz. Rumor had it that the Tirpitz was even more powerful than her sister ship, the legendary Bismarck. Early in the war, she had gotten loose in the Atlantic and the Navy had had to chase her down. The Tirpitz had been hiding up there in Norwegian fjords all along, a looming threat of destruction to the all-important convoys to Russia. For that reason, the Home Fleet remained in Scapa, watching the Tirpitz.

The Navy had acknowledged they'd made a number of attacks on the Tirpitz, but their only success had been about a year previously, in September of 1943, using midget submarines. Four of the Navy's submarines each towed a midget submarine, always submerged during daylight. These surfaced at night to recharge their batteries, all fifteen hundred miles from Scotland to the entrance to Altenfjord, Norway near North Cape; the most northerly land in Norway. En route, two of the midgets and their two-man crews were apparently lost, but the other two entered the fjord and travelled submerged under their own power the rest of the way to Kaafjord, where the Tirpitz was anchored. There, still undetected, the two men from each boat managed to attach both of the one-thousand-pound explosive charges they'd brought with them to its hull. The four of them then went on board the Tirpitz, surrendered and waited for the explosions.

I was amazed at the nerve. It had worked. The damage was severe enough to immobilize her until just recently.

Walter explained that he now suspected that the British believed the Tirpitz has been or soon would be repaired and might leave her lair in that fjord and go on a rampage in the Arctic Ocean. Therefore, it stood to reason that they'd planned another attack. And Walter believed that we were going to be in it.

It made sense to me, and I marveled again at the courage of those submariners. At least two of them had gotten a Victoria Cross. However, fear of the Tirpitz had preoccupied the British all through the war because they believed her to be so dangerous. If she got free, she could inflict a devastating amount of damage to the Murmansk convoys, and those supplies were still critical to the Russians. That was why the Admiralty had kept a major part of their fleet in the north, rather than sending ships to join the Americans in the Pacific.

By the time our conversation was finished, I had no doubt that we were going to be involved in attacking the Tirpitz.

That afternoon I had an opportunity to take a look at Kirkwall, the town that for so long had supported this famous naval base. With several other officers and men from the Nabob, we went by our ship's boat to the battleship, the King George V, which was functioning as a way station. There, we waited on deck for a long time. Not once did any of the KG's officers even say as much as hello. In twos, they marched up and down the deck past where we were waiting as if they were on parade; one even marched holding a telescope under his arm, clearly oblivious of us being present. Once I had to move quickly out of his way; else I'm sure the exercising man would have walked right over me. Obviously, we didn't exist. They were not friendly types at all. It was an extreme contrast to the way we'd been received on the USS Houston. Fortunately, a lighter finally came by and took us to the shore.

Scapa Flow itself is simply a large body of water, circumscribed by two large islands and quite a number of smaller ones, beginning about six miles off the northern tip of Scotland. I already knew that those islands, the Orkneys, had a history dating back to Neolithic times, but that was not my interest this day. These low-lying islands were largely treeless. Such trees as there were leaned at an acute angle, apparently because of the strong autumn winds and the gales of the winter. Apart from the charm of the old stone buildings, an impressive cathedral, the stone homes and the stores, even the pubs, were stark and austere, not a place designed for rest and relaxation. The Scapa Flow community was committed to fighting the war on the seas. That had been its role in World War I, and now, in World War II, it had again taken up the mantle. Its atmosphere was cold and austere. This was not my kind of place, and I didn't linger.

After dinner that evening, I began to hear rumors about where we were going and what we were going to do after we got there. The first and most complicated one came from of all people, Schoolie. By this time, he and I had bunked together for some months and were as close as my former college roommate and I were. He confided that he'd heard we were going to take a convoy to Murmansk. Knowing that in addition to his teaching duties, he also deciphered signals, I decided he must be setting me up. I baited him, "I suppose that news just came in the latest cipher," knowing full well that he would never divulge any information he'd obtained from that source.

With a perfectly straight face, he told me that he had received it from a really reliable source, one of the stokers in his math class, who said he'd heard it from one of the gunners, who had connections.

"Are you sure that story didn't float into your head this morning as you did your morning acrobatics?" I asked. By this time, he was really good at swinging down from his upper bunk.

The next day, 17 August, two quite different officers came on board to speak to our aircrew in the Ready Room. We were never told their names. Bobby introduced the first by explaining that this gentleman was a Prisoner of War Specialist, and we had to listen to what he had to say.

His initial words were: "Gentlemen, I want to remind you officers that if you're captured, you're duty bound to try to escape."

Those words, together with the expression on his face and the intensity with which he spoke, alerted all of us that he had something he wanted to tell us. The room became very quiet as the story came together.

After he'd been shot down, he'd become a prisoner of war in a camp for Allied Naval Personnel. He'd expected that it would be pretty boring, but he'd soon discovered that he was wrong. The prisoners had developed an on-going elaborate escape organization, and everyone was involved. Some made maps, others made identification papers, and still others made clothing to be used after escaping. In addition, everyone had a role in digging tunnels and disposing of the unwanted earth. One of the ways was to have a tube inside one of their pant legs. After filling it with dirt, they would walk around the grounds, slowly releasing it, scuffing it in, and making sure the colour of the released material matched that of the ground.

As he related this, he did the slow shuffle they used. It looked funny, sort of like what Charlie Chaplin used to do. We all laughed, releasing some of the tension that had built up.

Of course, the guards had noticed how much walking they did, often commenting on what an active group they were, always walking. They'd even asked them why they walked in this peculiar style.

Smiling, he related how, at one time, they had three different tunnels. The Germans were not stupid and were sure they were tunneling, yet they couldn't find them. They had one tunnel that they'd already abandoned and thought they could use it to trap one of their officers, thinking he might be useful. One of them agreed to tell one of their junior officers about this tunnel. His reward was a promotion and two weeks' leave. But when he returned, he was so afraid that the prisoners would tell his superior officers the real story of how he'd found the tunnel that he provided them with lots of useful information and even hard-to-get material objects.

One of the tunnels was quite long—at least one hundred and fifty yards. It was also deep; about thirty feet, and as the soil was quite sandy, they had to shore virtually every bit of it. Because of its depth and length, they rigged lighting and ventilation systems, using electricity from the camp's supply. This tunnel was the one our guest had used when, at last, it became his turn to attempt to escape. He'd entered the tunnel not long after midnight. At first, everything had gone well, but when he was not quite halfway through, there had been an air raid and the electricity was turned off. The blackness was total. He couldn't see a damn thing. Groping his way forward, he'd touch one wall and then the other. His progress was excruciatingly slow. Sometimes he couldn't be sure in which direction he was going, but there was no going back. He had to go forward. After a while, he began to wonder if it would still be dark when he got out. It seemed like forever, but finally he reached the end and pushed the cover over the tunnel aside. It was still dark. He climbed out, replaced the cover, and then ran faster than he'd ever run before or since. He told us that it was a bloody relief to get out of that tunnel.

He stopped talking, fished in a pocket, pulled out a packet of Players, lit one and took a deep drag and took several more deep drags while he walked quickly back and forth. Suddenly he stopped, butted his cigarette and began to talk. I wondered if in telling his story, he relived some of the emotions that he'd had during his escape.

He'd been disguised as a Hungarian naval officer, Count Gabor Buggeroff, which helped, as his German was very limited. However, he had all the appropriate travel documents and identification papers and enough German money. Still, he was very careful, travelling at night

CHARLES HERBERT READ JR

and hiding by day. He finally got to Hamburg, waited for a night when there was no moon, and managed to slip onto a Swedish ore carrier. He'd planned to hide in a lifeboat, but one of the crew saw him and told him not to, as Germans always inspected the lifeboats and their contents before letting them sail. The crewman had led him down to the very bottom of the ship to a space between a steel plate that supported the boiler and the steel of the ship's hull. It was just big enough for him to crawl into.

During the twelve-hour trip across the Baltic, our guest had roasted on one side and froze on the other. But he survived, landed in Stockholm, and went to the British Embassy. A few days later, a Royal Air Force Mosquito picked him up and flew him back to the U.K.

He finished his speech, thanked us for listening, distributed survival kits, made a couple of comments about them, and left. There was no opportunity for any of us to talk with him.

Later I opened the survival kit he'd given me. Enclosed in a firm clear plastic, measuring about six by eight inches and one inch thick, were items, including hard candy, a map of Norway printed on silk cloth, and a razor. He'd said that the razor was vital because all Norwegian men are clean shaven and the Germans would immediately suspect anyone who hadn't shaved that day. I attached my kit to my life preserver, thinking it was unlikely that I would be ashore in Norway, but one never knows.

I'd known that there were escape organizations in prison camps, but this was the first time I'd ever heard about one from somebody who'd actually been in one and had escaped. I thought he was one cool customer, and I wondered how well I would have coped under similar circumstances.

The second speaker that morning was very different—a three-ring British naval paybob commander. A man of some years and formidably proper, he lectured us in a very British accent about how to conduct ourselves and what to expect when we arrived in Murmansk. Russian officers would undoubtedly come on board, he told us. We were to be friendly and offer them food and as much liquor as they wanted. On the other hand, we were not to drink ourselves, as to avoid loose lips. Anything they wanted to see, we were to show them, but if they asked us anything about what they were looking at, we were to tell them that it's somebody else's department and that we didn't know anything about it.

He intimated that these instructions came from the very highest authority, perhaps someone who did not wholly trust the Russians. I wondered if he could be meaning Churchill, because one of my friends in a Canadian Bomber squadron in Yorkshire had told me, when I'd seen him briefly in Edinburgh, that they had received identical advice when they'd hosted a Russian Air Squadron. Their advice also had come from the highest authority. They too had assumed that was Churchill.

One of the things this speaker said was of special interest to me. Looking squarely at me, the only medical officer present, he explained that here, everyone knew that we were doctors by the red stripes between the gold ones on our sleeves. However, in Russia, it was the paybobs (accountants) who had the red stripes and the doctors who had the white ones. If we went ashore, we probably wouldn't be treated in the friendly way we were used to. The smirk on his face gave me the feeling he hoped it would be that way.

That afternoon, when I was telling Schoolie about the lectures I'd heard that morning, the shrill whistle of the bos'n pipe sounded, followed by the message, "All hands, cheer ship."

Schoolie, as surprised as I, said, "What the hell does that mean?" I certainly didn't know. Virtually everybody ignored it, as far as I could tell. It was not repeated, but my curiosity got the better of me, so I went up to the flight deck. Nobody was cheering. I looked around and through the haze, I could barely see a battleship slowly heading out to sea, accompanied by a bevy of destroyers. Soon I got the story. Early in the war the British battleship, Royal Sovereign, had been badly damaged and had been taken to America for repairs. On its return to Scapa Flow, the British turned it over to the Russians, who renamed her Archangel. Now she was leaving for Murmansk with a Russian crew. Having this ship, the Russians would now be able to participate in protecting the convoys carrying critically needed supplies to their northern ports. The order, "Cheer Ship," meant our ship's company was supposed to go up on deck, wave our hats in the air and cheer. Fat chance, I thought, that a Canadian crew would carry out such a ridiculous order, especially when they knew nothing about the ship and which could hardly be seen through the haze. A perfunctory recognition of protocol, I supposed.

As was our custom after morning Sick Call, Walter and I worked with our SBAs reviewing various medical techniques, making sure our supplies were in order, and ensuring our operating room was ready for immediate use. Afterwards I went up to my primary action station, the small medical first-aid room located just off the catwalk on the starboard side, immediately below the flight deck and forward of the place where I stood while our planes landed. It was ready, the supplies appropriate, stored properly, and easily available. My secondary action station was in the canteen deck, but we had decided not to store any supplies there.

After lunch, I heard that various members of the squadron had formed two teams and were going to play deck hockey on the flight deck. I asked Schoolie what he knew about it. He explained that it was field hockey. It was a game played at some private girls' schools in Canada, with rules similar to soccer.

What I saw certainly didn't look like a game that girls would be playing or one that I'd want to be playing either. Organized mayhem, perhaps would describe what they were doing. These young men were running at full speed up and down the deck, trying not to trip over the arrestor wires that stretched across the deck, all the while chasing a puck made of wood, four inches square with a one-inch thick cloth covering, presumably to keep it from breaking apart from the bashing it was getting from the curved four-foot hockey sticks the players were swinging with abandon. But the abuse the puck was receiving was nothing compared to the battering the players' shins were getting in the heat of battle. Nor were these protected shins, for few of the combatants had bound magazines to their lower legs.

Among the most active of the players was none other than Bobby Bradshaw, dressed, as were the others, in scuffs. He gave no quarter, nor did he receive any. For all intents and purposes, he was just one of the boys.

The next day the pace of activities increased, suggesting our sailing date was close. It was a hectic scene as tenders bringing supplies, drew alongside and discharged their cargoes. A small tanker topped off our fuel supplies. By late afternoon, they'd completed their various missions and one after another they headed back to their bases, their crews shouting things like, "Screw the bastards" or "Give them hell, Nabob" and, of course, "Good luck."

With all this evidence that we were about to sail, I was sure that the mood in the wardroom both before and after dinner that night would be upbeat. We always sang a lot on such occasions and this was a very special one. We had come to depend on Don Cash at the piano for parties such as this was likely to be, because we always enjoyed his great playing and his enthusiastic participation. The problem now was he was still in the hospital after flying into the Irish Sea on the night of 28 July.

By asking around, I found a very accomplished replacement. Everyone in the lower decks already knew of Tony Ticker, an AA3 in the squadron, and his unusual ability to play both dance music and everything else; I found out that he was even known as "Tick on Nabob." More of the ship's officers and aircrew than usual were present, and from the first moment they heard Tony play, they were in full voice; they also saw to it that Tony never had an empty glass. I was nominally in charge of the bar but, of course, it was Chizy, the wine steward, always cheerful, efficient and co-operative, who ran the show. Later on, I found out that he was rated as a Sick Berth Attendant. I have no idea why; he certainly never functioned as a part of our medical staff.

From the beginning, the party was upbeat. Encouraged by possibly more drinks than usual, we stood and sang with gusto. Tony knew every song we asked for, starting with *Roll A Long Wavy Navy, Roll A Long*, to the Fleet Air Arm *A Twenty-Five*. Tony went on playing many others, such as *McNamara's Band* and on and on, some quite ribald. I think he included Vera Lynn's entire repertoire, finally closing with *You'll Never Know, Dear, How Much I Love You*, his signature piece. It was a very special evening.

Chapter Seventeen

A Noble, if Tragic, Tradition

The next day, 18 August, we sailed. That morning, for the first time, I heard officially that our target was indeed the Tirpitz. Walter had been briefed about it and told me the operational plan. The whole operation had the code name Goodwood. We were part of a much more complex operation than I had imagined.

The German submarine fleet had suffered very heavy losses in the Atlantic in the past two years because of the new and improved tactics from the Allied side. In spite of this, at least ninety U-boats were known to be active in the Norwegian Sea and along the coast of Norway. A Killer Group, consisting of a flotilla of five warships, had already sailed in order to clear the way for us. Within the last two days, two German torpedoes had hit one of them, the Kite, which sank with a heavy loss of life. The very next day, depth charges from one of the planes from that group's aircraft carrier, the Vindex, destroyed that submarine.

However, our risk was still high. The hydrophones of the remaining four ships had confirmed the presence of many other U-boats. We were sailing through dangerous waters.

There were several other groups of our ships in this plan, all operating under one command, and they were all headed for the Arctic Ocean north of Norway. Then, after we finished off the Tirpitz, we were going to join a convoy of thirty-three merchant ships, together with two tankers and its escort of four corvettes, and go on to Murmansk.

We, in the Nabob, along with the Trumpeter, the heavy cruiser Kent, and five destroyers, were the Assault Group. But the really big power resided in the Home Fleet, where the admiral was flying his flag in the battleship Duke of York. With her were three fleet carriers, the

CHARLES HERBERT READ JR

Indefatigable, the Formidable, and the Furious, two cruisers, and six destroyers, one of which was the Canadian HMCS Algonquin. We were to be within visual signaling distance of the group, and we were all to maintain radio silence.

After listening to Walter, I realized we were going to be at the center of a really big show. I hoped it would work out as planned, but there were many pieces to it, and something could easily go wrong. I decided to go up to the flight deck and relax. There I stood, watching these fully camouflaged, powerful warships drive relentlessly onward at our slow cruising speed of fifteen knots.

It was both a surreal and a grand day. The baby blue of the cloudless sky contrasted with the dark blue of an ocean disturbed only by an occasional white cap and the white bow waves of the ships. In peaceful times, we might well have been sipping a long cool drink and admiring the scenery along the coast of Norway. On this day, that coast with its hostile German eyes was far distant. We even carefully avoided Shetland and Faroes. We were taking no chances of being prematurely discovered; surprise was so critical. We were part of a noble, if tragic, tradition. Countless fleets like ours had sallied forth on comparable missions, some of which ended successfully, others much less so. Now it was our turn, and we would face whatever was coming with all the courage we could muster. It was our turn to step into the middle of the action and do our part. We had a job to do, and we would do it, no matter the cost.

While I was stretching my legs on the flight deck the next day, I noticed that the Duke of York had hoisted a flag indicating the fleet was to make a ninety degree turn to port. All of the ships, including the Nabob, hoisted an identical flag, showing that they had all seen the signal. When the flagship's flag dropped, all the ships turned ninety degrees to port in unison. Well, not all. The Nabob turned ninety degrees to starboard and sailed off all by herself, in exactly the opposite direction.

We were, to a one, utterly mortified.

I knew exactly what those snobbish British in the other ships would be saying or thinking as they snickered, "Colonials, what do you expect?" For us Canadians, independent for over seventy years, to be called Colonials was insulting. They were fighting words; even if said as a joke, they were never a joke.

To get my mind off that, I decided to find out as much as I could about the impending attack on the Tirpitz, but the more I learned, the more I worried about our aircrew. Looking at reconnaissance photos, I saw that the Tirpitz, protected by anti-torpedo nets, was anchored very near the shore of the mountain in Kaafjord, the inland end of Altenfjord. A Messerschmitt 109 fighter squadron was stationed nearby, ready to defend their charge. With its fearsome array of weapons, the Tirpitz had extracted a heavy toll on her previous attackers. Situated and defended as she now was, she would be an even more formidable target. Was this attack going to be another Charge of the Light Brigade?

After dinner that evening, I had a talk with Parky, Bobby's navigator and right-hand man. I told him of my growing concern about the upcoming attack. A man of medium height, a few years older than the other men in the squadron, he had a pleasant but assertive outgoing personality, a great sense of humor and a strong Lancashire accent, which by this time I could understand. He told me about a meeting he'd attended in Northern Ireland back in July. Admiral McGrigor and his staff, who were responsible for northern operations, presented a plan for an attack on Tirpitz. Parky had been with Bobby, of course. The squadron leader of Squadron 856 and his observer from the Trumpeter were there too.

They'd listened as the admiral out-lined the proposed attack. First of all, 856 would make a diversion by making a dive bombing attack on Tirpitz, and then 852 would follow immediately, flying up the fjord and attack with two-thousand-pound mines. This time, they would be sure to finish that ship off.

Parky reminded me that neither he nor Bobby would hesitate to speak their minds at any time, even if they were surrounded by gold stripes. So he did, pointing out the flaw in their proposal. Their Avengers, as fine an aircraft as they were, when carrying a two-thousand-pound mine, would be slowed to about one hundred and fifty knots. With the heavy concentration of anti-aircraft guns that they all knew were lining the fjord, the chances were nil that any of the planes would ever reach the Tirpitz.

Admiral McGrigor had been surprised and somewhat taken aback that a two-thousand-pound mine would slow those aircraft down that much.

His aide, who was a three-ring commander and a pilot, had confirmed Parky's assessment.

From there, the admiral decided that they would have to re-think the whole plan.

The next day was 21 August and we were at 71 degrees north, 19 degrees east, which was about one hundred miles off North Cape, Norway, the northernmost land in Europe. I knew that this was about where we were going to launch our strike, being approximately 150 miles to where the Tirpitz lay hidden in Kaafjord. So far, the trip had been uneventful, the seas relatively calm with very little rain, though the skies had often been cloudy. As far as we could determine, the Germans had not yet detected us, but I privately felt that that was almost too good to be true. A fleet this large would be hard to hide, especially with all those German submarines about.

Earlier that morning, Bobby and Parky and presumably a similar pair from the Trumpeter, had flown to the flagship, the Indefatigable. There, Admiral McGrigor and his staff briefed the leaders of the two squadrons on the details of the revised plans for the attack. I didn't see Bobby or Parky when they first got back, but I heard several conflicting reports. One or two of the crew said Bobby looked very pale, which I found hard to believe. Walter said that was nonsense, but he did say they both looked very serious.

Many years after all of this, when Parky and I were old men, he told me a story. He claimed that prior to briefing the squadron for the attack on the Tirpitz, Captain Lay sent a message to Bobby and Parky, saying he wanted to see them in his day cabin. I knew nothing of what was said at the time; it wasn't until many years after the war that Parky told me about it and which I have had a hard time believing. When they arrived, the captain produced a signal he said he'd just received from the Admiralty and gave it to Bobby without comment. Bobby read it silently. As he did, Bobby's face tightened and his lips compressed and when he finished it, he looked very angry. Passing the message to Parky, he'd asked, why those stupid bastards at Admiralty would choose to send a signal like this, even before the operation had begun? And why would the captain think it was necessary for them to see it? The message had read, "Because we anticipate ninety-five percent losses of the two squadrons when they attack the Tirpitz, we already have designated two squadrons to replace them."

Parky told me that Bobby, ordinarily a very cool person, was boiling, probably more about the Admiralty having sent the signal than its contents. After all, he'd already heard the briefing on the Indefatigable just a short time ago, so he probably too anticipated such an outcome. As hopeful as we all were, we understood the realities of war. Not all of us would make it home. It was worse for pilots. A very precious few survived to have long careers during wartime. A tail gunner, the guy who rode in the tiny box at the rear of the plane to defend the craft from attack, had a life expectancy of about five missions.

I certainly thought this was an extraordinary thing for the captain to have done, choosing that moment to tell Parky and Bobby about that message, and at that moment I wondered if Parky might have made it up in his old age. I had no way to verify his story, but I doubted it, for it didn't fit with our going on to Murmansk after the attack on the Tirpitz if we wouldn't have any aircraft. Nor could I think of a single reason the captain would choose to share that message with anyone. Finally I decided that it was totally out of character for Captain Lay to do such a thing.

When Parky continued, however, he made more sense. He told me how, after the captain told them this, he summoned the aircrew to his day cabin on the hangar deck. This was apparently for them to see a large-scale relief model of Altenfjord, and its inland continuations, one of which was Kaafjord and the surrounding territory.

Bobby then took over and explained that he'd arranged for this because he wanted them to see the model of the target area so they'd have a better idea of what the territory was like that they were going to be flying over. As soon as they'd seen as much of it as they wanted, they would go to the ready room for the briefing.

At the briefing, Bobby was wearing the well-worn khaki army battle jacket he'd acquired during the months he'd flown in the desert campaign. He first told his men about the original plan and how they managed to put the kibosh on that one. This one, he assured everyone, was a little better. Although they were not going to fly the length of the fjord and be clay pigeons for the Germans, it was still going to be a shaky do, sort of a Victoria Cross action or nothing.

They were going to fly this circuitous route, while aircraft from the fleet carriers were causing a diversionary uproar over Altenfjord and Kaafjord to amuse and confuse their ack-ack and cross the coast. They would go inland from there, flying southeast until they were about opposite the Tirpitz, then swing west. Squadron 856 would be leading, so they would just have to follow them. Bobby showed them how the Tirpitz was anchored to the far side of the fjord, with the mountain rising steeply behind her. On the near side it was protected by anti-submarine nets. What they had to do was to drop their mines so that they fell in the space between the ship and the shore. They knew it was not going to be easy. But if they did it with those two-thousand-pound mines, it would put her out of commission for a long time. To Bobby's best calculations, they would only be over the fjord about fifteen seconds. His last words were a warning that there was a Messerschmitt squadron nearby, so everyone was to keep an eye out for them. He wished everyone the best of luck, and that was that.

The airmen seemed to take this daunting challenge in stride. They'd made copious notes and asked several times about judging the release point for dropping the mines. That could well be very difficult, because the Germans had always filled the fjord with smoke during an attack. The aircrew's questions showed that they recognized this was a difficult and dangerous mission.

After I left them, I decided to make one more check of the safety equipment on the aircrafts. This I needed to do because in late July, I'd learned that another of my roles was that of Air Safety Officer. Immediately, I'd made an inspection that made me very sensitive to the importance of this responsibility. I'd found that every single one of the large M-type rafts, big enough for three persons, that were supposed to be stored in a compartment on the port side of the aircraft, were missing. These aircraft had been flying, day after day, over the ocean and had not had this critically important piece of safety equipment. Fortunately, there had been no ditchings. I soon found the missing rafts, tucked away in a corner. I watched as crewmen stowed them in their proper place on each aircraft.

I'd also found why they had been removed from the planes. When Captain Lay and his golfing companions had gone ashore at Bangor, his barge had too deep a draft to allow it to go all the way in, so they used these rafts to complete the journey. But he'd never given orders to have the rafts put back where they belonged. I was very angry about this and talked to Walter. We finally decided that the only thing that we could do was to add it to the goof list that someday we would report at some appropriate time to higher ups.

When I checked the aircraft again, I found the rafts properly stowed, the windscreens scrupulously clean, the parachutes recently inspected, and the K-type personal dinghies in place. As far as I could determine, all the aircraft's personal safety equipment was in order.

With the attack now less than twenty-four hours away, I was very much on edge, especially because the signals we were receiving from the flagship were suggesting doubt about whether the attack would go forward the next day. I didn't know what was causing these doubts. I just knew that the element of surprise was very important, for the sooner we attacked, the less chance there was of us being discovered.

The night wore on.

No decisions.

Chapter Eighteen

The Quick and the Dead

Hour by hour, I kept in touch with the situation, undoubtedly making a nuisance of myself in doing so. Increasingly, I doubted whether these admirals in charge, who were presumably making the decisions, knew what the hell they were doing at all. I knew that many of the senior naval officers of that day belonged to the battleship generation. Did they really know anything about modern naval air war? I didn't understand why they refused to talk to the Americans, who were so successfully using large-scale naval air power in the Pacific. As for Lay, his two weeks with the America Navy seemed woefully inadequate. I wondered why he didn't ever go back for more information before he took the Nabob to sea.

Finally, to relieve my tension I went up on the flight deck. It was after midnight, but since we were well north of the Arctic Circle, it was still light enough to see the other ships of our fleet steadily pressing onward. As I walked up and down the length of the deck at the same unhurried pace, men from the aircrew joined me for short periods. We shared stories about our families back home, the Kiwis always talking about how wonderful New Zealand was. They certainly made me want to visit that country, way off in the western Pacific. Without exception, they talked about how much they loved their home country, how beautiful it was, how much they admired Bobby and how lucky they felt that they were in the 852 Squadron.

They seemed to have accepted me as their friend and confidant. I felt good about this and thought that might be in part because in the aviation medicine course I'd learned to speak their language as well as done many of the things they'd done, like enjoyed aerobatics, experienced anoxia in a decompression chamber, and flown as a passenger on and off our ship, as well as conducted that relatively long trip with Bobby and Parky. Then too, they were probably very aware that I was always standing in the starboard catwalk by the first arrestor wire for every take-off or landing in my emergency medicine role. They knew I'd lifted the unconscious Don Cash from the destroyer's lifeboat, carried him up the side of the ship to the hangar deck, and subsequently operated on him. They also knew I'd looked after Gavin Waite when he'd been injured by the slithering arrestor wire. They'd seen that I supported them and that I'd been there to help them. Maybe they'd decided I was an okay doc. Finally, I decided it was really because they were such a fine group of intelligent young men. I had come to like them very much, and I certainly wished them well on tomorrow's mission. I fervently hoped they would all survive, but I was worried. I was very conscious that the aircrew of these two squadrons were doing what I had envisioned those years ago when, immediately after the war began, I wanted to attack Hitler and the Nazis myself and was deferred by Dr. Penfield's advice to become a doctor. Now, I was looking after all these men who were about to risk and, for some, sacrifice their lives.

Bearing this in mind, I continued to monitor the situation throughout the night to make sure the aircrew would not be disturbed unless they were going to fly. Finally, about 0600, I learned a decision had been made. The fly-off would be at 0700. I went about making sure everyone knew. Then I visited the cooks to make sure breakfast for the aircrew would be ready and include juice, bacon and eggs, toast, marmalade and coffee or tea; these were the breakfast foods these men liked and insisted upon before flying in the morning.

Even before 0700, some were in the ready room. I thought this would be the period of greatest anxiety, for once they were airborne they would be so busy with their various tasks, any nervousness would disappear. As my action station was nearby, I was able to keep track of what was going on without being too intrusive.

When 0700 came and went and there was no further information, I lost more confidence in the admiral's competence. I wondered if it was the same Admiral McGrigor who had conducted the planning committee back in July. We all just waited and waited. Some of the aircrew read, some knitted, some crocheted, and others just sat and talked quietly. Each had his own way of coping with the situation. They had likely been through delays like this many times before. I thought of how I had coped the many times I'd waited for my father when I was his summertime chauffeur.

About 0830, I was talking with Walter when the captain announced that he'd just heard that one of the Wildcats protecting this fleet had shot down a German aircraft. Lay sounded jubilant. Throughout the ship, a great cheer went up. Walter didn't cheer. "Uh-oh," he said grimly. "Now we're in for it." Now the Germans knew where we were, and they would be after us.

I decided the best place to wait for the take-offs was the ready room. I found a comfortable chair and settled down to wait it out. Before long, came the words we'd been waiting for: "Pilots, man your aircraft."

The aircraft, fully fueled and armed, were ready. On the flight deck, I listened to the increasing roar of the engines as they revved up and noticed how the light mist accentuated the whirl of the propellers. The weather was clear and the fifteen-knot wind would be helpful for take-off.

We turned into wind, as did the Trumpeter. Everything was ready. Because of the heavy mine load, all the aircraft would have to be catapulted. The others, lined up on the deck, awaited their turn. When all were ready, the first aircraft was positioned on the catapult. Bobby ran the engine up to full power, checked the controls and told his crew to be ready. When the deck control officer waved his wand in a circular motion, Bobby gave the thumbs up to those on the bridge, and he braced his head against its support, anticipating the G force soon to come. Down came the wand and off went the plane, dipping toward the sea to gain airspeed before climbing in a port turn to the altitude at which they were going to form up. In quick succession, the flight deck crew moved in each of the remaining eleven aircrafts in turn to the catapult.

The fly-off went well, to my relief. I thought that the flight deck crew had done a good job moving these very large airplanes around and positioning them for the take-off. They were an outstanding unit and had always launched our aircraft more quickly than the Trumpeter's crew. Today was no exception.

During landing and take-offs, carriers had to hold a steady course directly into the wind to maximize the wind speed over the deck.

Completing these operations quickly was extremely important, for when not zigzagging, we became an easier target for a submarine's torpedo. Speed was everything. An inspecting admiral told us that with carriers, there were only the quick and the dead. Those who were not quick were soon dead.

Having reached their designated altitude, our squadron, joined by the Trumpeter's, circled overhead. Flying in tight V formations, their wings overlapping, the roar of their Pratt and Whitney radial engines increasing and decreasing they flew round and round, now closer, then farther away. As I watched, sometimes from the flight deck, more often from my usual place on the starboard catwalk opposite the arrestor wire, I noticed that no other aircraft had joined them. This wasn't what I'd expected. Why were the fleet carriers so slow getting their airplanes into the air? Only occasionally did one take off from their expansive decks. A half hour went by and though the sky seemed filled with our circling planes, no other planes had joined them. I wondered if they would have enough fuel to make my attack and return. Then, much to my surprise, we turned into wind and prepared to receive our aircraft. One after another they landed safely. I couldn't understand why they had come back.

The ship's crew remained at action stations; the aircrew returned to the ready room. I continued to be confused about the recall and thought perhaps the admiral and his group had messed things up.

From 1944 until 1993, when I learned that Don Cash had moved to Nova Scotia, I'd had no contact with 852 Squadron. The next year, he and I attended a reunion of the squadron in Sherborne. There, for the first time, I heard hints that we had not launched our squadron on 22 August. The Nabob book, published in 1989, but of which I had not previously heard, also stated that. But I had such a vivid, visual memory of those planes taking off, flying around and around and then landing back, that I dismissed these accounts as not being in accord with the facts. More recently, however, I asked Angus Weston and Bill Reeks about this. Both of them checked their log books. They both said there was no record of having flown on 22 August. Apparently, I must have fallen asleep in the ready room while waiting and dreamed the take-off and return.

I've found it very difficult to believe that I'd done so because it was all so vivid, but I've reconciled myself that having been already tired and up all that night, that I might indeed have fallen asleep.

At 1500, our Wildcats that had been flying fleet air protection landed. Shortly afterward, action stations were secured and we went to defense stations—a lower level of readiness with only half the crew at their action stations.

Our group, the Kent, the Nabob, the Trumpeter, and our escorts withdrew to the west, and we began preparing to fuel three of the destroyers, in the course of which it was necessary to pull our cat gear. This was a noise-making apparatus that trailed behind the ship, making it, rather than the ship, the target for acoustic torpedoes. None of our escorts reported sonar responses, but we didn't then know that in the frigid water of the Arctic, sonar was not reliable.

I watched two of the Trumpeter's Wildcats take off, taking over fleet air protection. Because everyone had been at action stations since early in the morning, no one had eaten and we were all hungry. The cooks had already gone to the galley to prepare food. Representatives from each of the messes got ready to join an escorting officer down to the rum locker, located deep in the bowels of the ship to draw rum for Up Spirits.

At about 1530, all the stresses and lack of sleep in the past thirty-six hours caught up with me. I knew I had to get some rest. I wanted to be as fresh as possible for whatever might happen next. I went to my cabin, pulled my chair close to my bunk, and draped my life jacket over the back of it so that it was already spread and easy to put on. I then took off my clothes and laid them on the seat of the chair in the order in which I'd put them on in an emergency. I arranged my shoes, not on the floor, but on the chair, where they'd be in easy reach. After I was fully undressed, I put on the orange silk pajamas I'd bought in New York to wear in especially dangerous situations. After a glass of orange juice, I quickly fell asleep.

Chapter Nineteen

One Hell of a Mess

The next thing I knew, I launched into the air amid the loudest noise I'd ever heard. Landing on my back, almost out of my bunk, I didn't need to hear the action gong to tell me something very serious had happened to the Nabob. My first guess was that we'd been torpedoed. We hadn't blown up, not yet anyway, but I needed to get to my action station, quickly.

In the darkness, I reached for and found the flashlight I'd attached to my lifejacket, turned it on and pulled my trousers and jacket on over my pajamas and stepped into my shoes. Thankfully, because of how I'd arranged them, I'd easily found my clothes. Socks could wait. I slipped into my lifejacket, put on my cap and, and using my flashlight to light my way, quickly walked the short distance to the nearest ladder on the port side which lead to the decks above. Even though I'd been sleeping just moments ago, I was entirely alert, both physically and mentally.

Fifteen or so of the crew and aircrew were already there, waiting for those who were coming along the companionway from aft in the ship to go up the ladder. Nobody spoke, and there was no evidence of any panic. I assumed that they, as I, were all intent on getting to their action stations or at least to the flight deck. We understood that we could take the time we needed for safety, but not a moment more. I decided that this would be a good opportunity to put on my socks. I'd wrapped a clean pair in a condom to keep them dry should I get in the water, and I'd fastened them to my lifejacket. I did that, my turn came, and I followed the others up the ladder.

22 August, 1944 Nabob Transmission: "1716.Torpedo starboard quarter."

Walter told me later that he'd noted in his diary, "I would guess that at 1710 we got fished, allowing those characters on the bridge time to figure what happened and to make up a signal."

Reaching the hangar deck, I wasted no time walking across to the starboard side, being careful to avoid parked aircraft. I noticed that they must have been well tied down, for none of them had budged from their positions. We were listing to starboard, our stern was almost under water, and our bow was sticking way up in the air. We were in one hell of a mess. The hangar deck had a bulge in it, but none of plates were cracked and the welding remained intact. My thoughts briefly went back to what Gus Airey had said about welded ships the first day I was on board, that if the welding held throughout the ship, the hull would probably remain unified. On the other hand, the same force might well have sprayed rivets everywhere and, in that event, we'd probably be rapidly sinking. However, so far, things were all right.

When I reached the enclosed ladder leading to the flight deck and my action station, I reminded myself that in the total darkness of its enclosed space, I would lose the major component to balance that sight supplies. Knowing that didn't help. After only a few steps, I had the feeling we were going to capsize. Expecting that at any moment I would be faced with a torrent of incoming water as the Nabob capsized, I went up those steps as if the devil was chasing me. Reaching the top step was not enough. Before going to my nearby action station, I simply had to go out on the catwalk to make sure we were still more or less upright.

On the flight deck, I looked out to starboard. I saw that one of our escorts was dead in the water. The rest of our fleet was high-tailing away from us, presumably at flank speed. For a moment, I thought they were abandoning us, but I immediately understood their need to get out of this danger zone.

The suffering escort was the destroyer Bickerton. Clouds of steam and smoke partially obscured her, but it looked as if her stern was badly damaged and even at this distance I could hear her siren wailing without ceasing. Apparently, the torpedo hit her just a few minutes after we caught our fish. Someone suggested she had sacrificed herself in an attempt to save the Nabob from a second one. But I thought a

Nazi Gnat torpedo had homed on her propeller while it was still turning, while ours were stopped. This turned out to be the case. Later on, one of our Asdic operators told me that we were damned lucky. We'd tracked three other torpedoes that missed everything. It turned out that they were ordinary torpedoes.

I went to my action station located just off the catwalk below the flight deck. It was a total mess, unusable. The examining table and other standing furnishings were overturned. The surgical instruments, bandages, tapes, broken bottles of saline, iodine, and Mercurochrome, once neatly stored in cabinets and drawers, lay in a colourful, chaotic mélange on the deck. Until it was cleaned up and re-stocked, it would be impossible to treat any patients there.

I returned to the flight deck to see if anyone needed help. By this time, many of the crew were standing on the port side. It wasn't likely that they thought their cumulative weight would have much of an effect, but perhaps they felt they were farther away from that black, cold water that surrounded us than when they were on the starboard side. I went around asking if anyone knew of anybody who'd been injured. Nobody did.

Then the stoker Petty Officer Jefferson came over to me, clad only in oil-covered underwear. He'd been busy oiling the propeller shaft when he'd been suddenly covered by oily water. Luckily, he'd found a hatch and managed to get out. He hadn't wanted to keep wearing the uniform. He seemed quite unfazed by his experience. Incredible, I thought, that he was so calm, having had such a narrow escape. I told him to go get some clothes.

Another rating came up to me, stark naked and holding a bar of soap. I wanted to know where his clothes were, and why he was holding soap. Apparently, he'd been in the shower when we'd been hit, so he'd decided that he'd best come right up to his action station.

I told him that if his quarters were not flooded down there, he should go some clothes on; if they were, he should get some from somebody. He needed to be clothed for whatever might happen next.

As there seemed to be no need for my services up on the flight deck, I decided to go down to my secondary action station in the canteen flats, a deck or so below where my cabin was located. By this time, I'd figured out that was near the area where the torpedo had struck. I had little enthusiasm and some considerable anxiety about going down there, but someone may be needing medical assistance, and the rendering of such was my primary purpose in this man's navy. Whether I wanted to go had nothing to do with my decision to go; it was my duty to go there. If I didn't, I would have forever labeled myself a coward. That was not a burden I wanted to bear for the rest of my life.

I crossed to the port side to avoid flooding, descended three decks, and walked toward the stern until I reached the canteen flats. Once there, my misgivings disappeared; I was calm and alert, certain as to what I was doing. It was quite a shock to see the canteen. Ordinarily, it was brightly lit and filled with crew members talking, eating, playing cards, or just resting; now I was the only one there, and it was quiet, wet, and dark. The only light was from my flashlight and the reflections upon black oily water that covered the deck absorbed most of its light. However, I was able to see that because of our list, the water level varied from one or two inches where I was standing to a much higher level on the starboard side. Some hours later, when Walter went down on the starboard side, he said the water was up to his knees or even higher. Looking aft toward the galley, it appeared as if the deck had torn loose on the starboard side and curled over to port side, while the steel netting separating the galley from the canteen flats was torn and, at the top, bent forward. Looking into the galley as best I could, I saw the kettles and galley equipment had scattered all about. There was no sign of life, nor could I see any bodies. But with that amount of damage, some of the cooks must have been badly hurt or worse. Unfortunately, I couldn't find any way to get into the area.

1734 To Nabob from Vigilant. "Following received from C and C addressed to Kempthorne, Kent. Vigilant: sink Bickerton and unless Nabob can steam sink her also."

Walter told me that he'd noted in his diary, "C and C didn't waste any time. Probably interrupted his tea hour."

Through with my inspection, I thought I heard the captain's voice come over the intercom. I could barely hear him. I thought he'd told us to prepare to abandon ship, but I couldn't be sure. I did wonder what one did to prepare to abandon ship. It was an odd order. Maybe it was just abandon ship. Anyway, I hadn't finished looking around. I knew that I might still find someone who I could help, so I just ignored whatever he'd said.

After I completed my inspection of the canteen area, I walked forward on the companionway leading to the sick bay, and began to wonder if we were abandoning ship. A breathless seaman ran up to me and told me that Lieutenant Goad was in his cabin and had clear fluid running from his nose.

Goad's cabin was forward on the same deck and not far. My first thought was that he'd had a head injury involving his cribriform plate (a thin layer of bone separating the brain from the nasal cavity). That fluid could be cerebrospinal fluid.

I ran to his cabin.

Much to my surprise, he was standing in front of a mirror tying his tie, in no apparent distress. Moreover, he had on his very best uniform, the one worn only on special occasions, complete with a new clean white shirt. He appeared calm and alert. While making a quick visual inspection of him, I asked why he was all dressed up. He certainly didn't look as if he'd been injured.

He calmly told me that not long after they'd stood down from Action Stations, he'd mustered the representatives of the various messes so they could draw rum for up spirits. Harold Chizy, our great wardroom steward, had come along to get some supplies. They had just arrived there and everyone but he had gone into the rum locker when the sea came in on us. The water had tossed him around violently, but after a bit he'd found himself floating up against the deck-head, his head in a bubble of air. The air had become stale, and he'd found another bubble in the next section. It too had become stale, so he'd started what he recognized as a life or death search for another. His lungs had been about to burst when he'd come to an open hatch and he'd shot up through it a like a cork and then through another open one on the deck above. Fortunately, he'd taken his life jacket off when he first got down there. Taking off the jacket had slowed him so he hadn't been in the locker when we'd been hit. If he hadn't taken it off, he never would have been able to get through those openings. Then he'd come along here to get some dry clothes. He decided he might as well dress completely while he was at it, and the only other uniform he had was this one; his number ones.

All this he said in a calm, detached voice, as if it might have happened to somebody else. His discarded wet clothes lying on the deck supported his remarkable story.

I checked his pupils, looked for signs of head trauma; there were none. I tasted the fluid that was still dripping from his nose; it was as salty as sea water. As far as I could tell, he was okay. Presumably pressure had forced sea water into his sinuses. Now they were draining.

Sick dread curled through my stomach as I realized what Goad's story meant. There was a whole party of men in that rum locker, among them was Chizy, the affable wine steward who had taught me the ropes of liquor rations and sales that first day I'd boarded the Nabob.

I didn't want to ask. I didn't want to hear what I already knew, but at moments like these, an officer's duty takes precedence over his own wants. So I inquired after the rest of Goad's party.

Although he didn't tell me anything I didn't know, my heart sank as Goad explained. They'd been ahead of him, already in the rum locker, and there was no way they could have escaped that pressure from the sea coming in on them.

Of the fourteen men in the group, Goad was the only survivor. I comforted myself with the thought that although drawing the rum rations was certainly not why they had joined the navy, but at least they were carrying out a long-established naval tradition and they had all volunteered to be in the party. Chizy had been a fine, intelligent young man; always helpful, always cheerful, and always carrying out his duties impeccably.

There was no time to grieve. I went to the sick bay to see if there might be some injured there. There wasn't a soul in sight, not even any tiffies. It was unlikely that we had no wounded. I wondered if they'd been taken somewhere else. Perhaps the prepare to abandon ship order had meant that wounded were already being evacuated to another ship. I went back to my cabin to pick up my 8mm movie camera. It still had a little film left unused in it. I also picked up a white shirt, but almost immediately discarded it, deciding that I didn't need a white shirt right then.

1745. To Kent from Nabob. "Am flooded up to the engine room and afraid bulkhead will not hold."

Rice noted in his diary that, "The engineers and shipwrights had reported. Lay didn't get below till a couple of days later. Some of his pals never did come down to the flight deck. Later I tried to get him to open up some life jacket stores, with no success. We did get the key in other ways, however."

When I got back on the flight deck, it was clear that from the number of sailors standing around that few, if any, had left the ship. I'd heard no further announcements relative to preparing to abandon ship, but I soon saw that the captain's order had been a major mistake. Apparently Captain Lay must have panicked and given a nonsensical order. I later learned that the order to prepare to abandon ship doesn't exist. It's either abandon ship or silence. So, as a result, all the Carly floats that had been lowered to the water and, not properly tethered, had floated away. This was potentially disastrous, for if now we had to abandon ship, most of us would be in the water and we all knew that the chance of anyone surviving for more than a few minutes in the frigid water of the Arctic Ocean was zero.

I saw Walter standing near the ladder to the bridge, so I walked over to talk to him and remarked how it hadn't taken the Germans too long to find us. I asked him about casualties.

Walter hadn't heard anything. He'd been in the wardroom when we were hit, and he'd gone straight to sick bay, which was his action station. There hadn't been a soul there, no injured, not even any of the tiffies. But he'd learned that the tiffies had collected casualties in the canteen flats area, so Walter had carried out emergency treatments and had taken them to a place on the starboard side of the hangar deck near the stern, where they could most easily be evacuated. When they'd heard the order to prepare to abandon ship, they'd decided to lower one to a waiting boat operated by Fog Buoy Fraser. Then they'd had a problem. A rope securing one of the four corners of the stretcher had come loose, dumping the patient in the water. Fraser had immediately jumped into the water, disentangled the patient and had gotten him into the boat. The patient was fine, according to Walter, but Fraser was blue for a long time afterward. The tiffies and patients had been taken to the Kempthorne.

They'd done damned well, and I was pleased. They'd carried out their duties without supervision, just as they'd been trained to do. I told Walter about Goad, the tragic fate of Chizy's party, and that I'd not been able to find anyone else who needed help.

From the very front of the flight deck I surveyed the scene. Fortunately, the sea remained relatively calm, but I was struck at how black it was, and how evil and inhospitable it looked. Off to our starboard lay the Bickerton, smoke still pouring from her ruptured inwards, her siren still wailing, obviously fatally wounded. I knew that those poor bastards must have had a lot of casualties. The Kempthorne was standing by her, taking off both her injured and the rest of her crew.

The only other remaining escort that I could see, the others having apparently accompanied the Trumpeter, seemed to be making square searches. Now with only the Kempthorne and the other destroyer to protect us from another fish, I knew that we were a sitting duck. To get this close to the British Home Fleet, the captain of the submarine was not only brave, but also an enterprising commander. I thought the probabilities were that he would not give up. I was sure that he would be waiting for another chance.

The rest of our fleet had long since disappeared over the horizon.

I was still watching the Kempthorne transferring the Bickerton's crew when Hills, the Anglican chaplain, came up to me. He, with his high arched eyebrows and beatific face, was pointing to his mouth, which he kept opening and closing as if he were talking, but from which no sound emitted. I did a quick examination of his neck and mouth. There were no abnormalities. Then the diagnosis dawned on me; he was trying to tell me he couldn't speak. This Man of Faith had lost his voice. I felt like asking him if he thought his God had deserted him in his time of peril. Instead I said, "Chaplain Hills, if you ever again stand on dry land, I'm sure your voice will return." From what I knew of the crew's opinion of him, I don't think many would care.

We were lucky to be still afloat. Considering all the high-octane aviation fuel we had on board and those depth charges and other munitions, I could not comprehend how we'd not blown up.

We'd had no further word about abandoning ship. From my position standing at the front of the flight deck and looking aft, it seemed the attitude of the ship was about the same, the stern barely above water, the bow high in the air and the ship listing fifteen degrees to starboard. Nothing seemed to be happening. Even more of the crew were clustered on the port side than when I first came topside, standing singly or in groups, talking quietly, waiting. At no time had I seen any sign of panic. But it seemed to me only a matter of time before we would hear the order to abandon ship, and with virtually all our survival equipment having floated away, not many of us would survive.

I had already accepted the inevitability of my own death; it was not a matter of whether, only of when. In no way did this alarm me. I was deeply calm, having previously divested myself of the shackles of orthodox religion because I'd come to realize that I couldn't believe anything for which there was no proof. I did feel disappointed I was not going to do the things I'd hoped to do in the future, including have a family, live in peace, seek knowledge, and serve mankind, probably as a pediatrician. I was sorry for my parents and Anne, with whom I'd shared only two years of marriage. They would be distressed. But they all knew I had voluntarily accepted the risk when I joined the navy, and that I had felt strongly that it was of the utmost importance that the forces of Nazism be defeated, and that I wanted to play a part in it. I had no other regrets.

Just then a stoker rushed up to me, interrupting my reverie, telling me that Len Love had gone down to the diesel room to get his friend George Meredith, and neither of them had returned. I agreed to go with him to check if they were all right.

I followed him down several decks to the diesel room. There we found the two men bending over some machinery, very much involved with what they were doing. They barely looked up when I asked if they were okay.

They were; they just had a job to get done. One of them was indeed Len and he asked me to hold the flashlight so he could see to work.

As he worked, he explained that when we got fished, the working diesel engine had quit, but he hadn't the foggiest idea why. But it meant no electricity anywhere in the ship, because the other diesel engine was already down for routine maintenance. The injectors were out, so he and George were trying to put the suckers back in.

I knew enough to recognize the importance of what they were trying to do. Without electricity there was no way the big generators could operate, and the fans that cooled the engine rooms would remain inactive. This meant that the temperature there (140) was too high for men to work in. The only hope for Nabob was to get a supply of electricity.

I tried to help by holding the flashlight Len had given me and added that of my own. In another few minutes, they got the injectors in and discontinued the speed control.

Ordinarily, we used two hundred pounds of compressed air to get the diesel engines started, but we had only eighty pounds left in the tank. We hoped it would be enough. It was a toss-up. If it didn't cut in by the second roll, we were finished.

I'm sure that we all held our breaths as George cranked and gave it the eighty pounds of air. It rolled over once and then, on the second roll, it cut in.

I'm not sure they even heard me, as they were already arranging for the electricians to make the switch to the engine room switch-board. Soon, the engine room fans would be back on. Then we'd find out whether, if everything else was intact, we could start the engines. It would also mean that there would be lighting throughout the ship, which would allow the damage control teams to better evaluate the problems and for the shipwrights to start shoring. Especially critical, I was told, was the bulkhead protecting the engine room from the flooded area in the stern.

By the time I got back to the flight deck, my spirits had risen considerably. Seeing a couple of the tiffies nearby, I joined them, asking if they were all right. They were. They hadn't seen any casualties, even though, as Hadley MacDowell told me, they'd looked everywhere. Hines and Carter had found some and evacuated them to the Kempthorne.

Henri Lebrun explained to me that they'd chosen to stay behind in case they were needed for something. He asked if I wanted some hot food.

I greatly appreciated the offer, but even though I hadn't eaten since breakfast, I seemed to have no desire for food, but I did have a few bites because I didn't want to turn down their offer.

1807. Nabob to Vigilant. "Carrying out observant round the ship. Kempthorne is picking up Bickerton's survivors. I am not abandoning ship yet and hope to remain afloat."

Walter's journal noted that, "The order to prepare to abandon ship, having led to the jettisoning of all the Carly Floats is now rescinded. That order was made about the time of the first signal."

About this time the captain, using a bullhorn, called out from the bridge that they thought there was a chance they might be able to save the ship if they could shore the engine room bulkheads. They needed volunteers to go down below to help the shipwrights get some shoring done.

Immediately, at least a hundred men stepped up. Each of the several times I'd gone down, I'd experienced less and less anxiety, but I'd spent relatively short times below doing what I had to do and I'd done so because I felt it was my duty. But these men were going down for probably extended periods with little hope of surviving if a bulkhead gave way. Of course, the stokers, the engineers, and damage control parties, who already were working below, shared the same danger, but their risks, like mine, were part of their job. But these men were different; they'd volunteered to expose themselves to a potentially real danger. There seemed no end to the number of brave and courageous men we had in our crew. I felt very proud of the way our ship's company was performing.

The appeal made to these men made me realize why we had all those six by six inch deals. All that lumber I'd seen being brought on board in New York and Belfast and neatly stowed away was to use for shoring. The thin steel walls of the bulkheads were not made to withstand the tremendous pressure of the seawater that now flooded the aft compartments.

1830. To Nabob From Kent. "I will return at 2130 to see how you are getting along. Meanwhile keep Vigilant and frigates in company with you for your own protection.

Rice's diary read, "C and C has ordered that if you cannot steam under your own power, you are to be sunk."

Chapter Twenty

Nothing by my Best

Soon after this, a seaman came up to me and told me I was to go to the Kempthorne immediately to look after the casualties who had been collected there. A boat was waiting for me.

One of our ship's boats delivered me to the side of the destroyer Kempthorne, where a scramble net hung down from its deck. Standing on the boat's gunnel, I grabbed the scramble net and began to pull myself upward on the sturdy hemp rope. I'd never done this before, and the climbing was far more difficult than I'd expected. About halfway up, I began to wonder if I could make it. Then I looked down for possible alternatives. The boat had moved away. Below me was that black, cold, evil-looking Arctic Ocean water.

I chose to keep climbing.

With renewed resolution, I began to claw my way upward. As I neared the deck, helpful hands grasped my wrists and pulled me up the last few inches and onto the deck. I was physically exhausted. Never have I been I more grateful than for the help I received in that last foot or so.

Someone led me down to a mess where ordinarily at least some of the crew slept and ate, situated immediately beside the Sick Bay. There, SBA Lebrun met me and said that Kempthorne's doctor, a young Irish surgeon, felt overwhelmed and had requested for another physician to join him so he could concentrate on those who required major surgery. He'd apparently been at it for some time and our PO Hines, SBA Carter, and some other of our SBAs were actively helping him. That was good news, especially when I learned he was a trained surgeon and undoubtedly had had a lot more experience in treating traumatic injuries than I.

The lighting in the mess was atrocious. I could hardly see the thirty or so injured men who seemed to be distributed willy-nilly around the periphery of the deck. Never in my training had I faced a situation even remotely like this. But this was not the time to think about whether I could cope; it was a job that had to be done and I would do nothing but my best. I was grateful that my favourite tiffies, Lebrun and MacDowell, were with me. The three of us began a triage, obtaining brief histories, doing what I thought were appropriate physical examinations and making decisions about the urgency of treating each of these patients.

No matter how seriously injured they were, none of these men complained. Over and over, I was told to look after the other guys first. Everyone wanted to wait for their buddies to receive care before they themselves did. Sometimes it was difficult to discover what their problems were. I was fortunate to have my flashlight, but even with it, the awful lighting in the mess made the whole procedure infinitely more difficult. We did the best we could, separating those who seemed to have the most urgent need for treatment. Fortunately, we had no active bleeding with which to cope, for we had neither blood for transfusions, nor as far as I knew, even any equipment for doing a cross-match. Several men were non-responsive and likely near death. We gave morphine to those in pain.

One petty officer from the Bickerton, said to have been decorated for bravery, was in a critical condition, seemingly from internal injuries. I thought there was chance we could save him, so I chose to treat him first. In retrospect, this was probably an error, because he was in shock, his blood pressure was difficult to measure, his pulse weak and thready. I tried to start an IV, but all of his veins were so collapsed I couldn't get a needle in. Then I did a 'cut-down' on his saphenous vein at the right ankle. I isolated the vein without difficulty, but it was so collapsed, the only way I could be sure it was a vein, was to make an incision in it and, using a syringe, push some fluids in. Compared to his need, the amount was trifling. All this probably took a relatively short time, but it seemed a very long time, and then it was evident he was dead.

I was shaken by what I viewed as my total lack of success with this patient; however, we had to move on to the others. They presented with a variety of problems, including second-degree burns, a fractured ankle, sprains, and lots of lacerations that needed to be stitched. We treated them, one after another until finally they'd all received care.

I had no idea what time it was when MacDowell, Lebrun, and I dragged ourselves up to the quarter deck of the Kempthorne and sat down on whatever was handy. Already the sun, partially obscured by fog, was well above the horizon. We didn't talk; we just sat there, exhausted, each probably deep in his own thoughts. After some time, we got up to go down to make a last check on our patients. Then MacDowell told us to look over to port. The Nabob was underway.

Indeed she was. The Nabob was moving, slowly, but plowing ahead, her stern barely visible, but her bow held high, as if proud of her achievement. She had survived the test of life or death. A thought ran through my head. Our ship may have been snake-bit, but her lucky number 77 had saved her. I wondered how the crew had done it, against such daunting odds. I just hoped they and 77 could keep her together enough to get her back to Scapa Flow. That was a long trip, about 1100 miles. I hoped we wouldn't have any bad storms, as she must have been finely balanced as she was.

I checked the sick bay; everything seemed to be under control. So I went to bed. The captain of the Kempthorne thoughtfully had arranged for me the use of his day cabin.

Later that morning, I attended the burial service, standing on the port side of the quarter deck.

In the beginning, I found it agonizing to watch, for while we'd done the best we could, we had not saved these men. In the beginning our successes, no matter how many or how significant, seemed to have disappeared or seemed inconsequential. But as the service came to a close, I began to regain perspective, realizing that all of us were participating in the same great cause, saving mankind from tyranny. It was for this cause that these men and many others had left behind everything and everyone. It now was for us, who by incredibly good fortune had survived to this day, to pick up their burden and carry it forward. As for me, I hoped that would be as a flight surgeon on another Canadian aircraft carrier. I hadn't done much to get rid of

Hitler and his followers so far, but I'd done as much as I could. Perhaps I would feel better if I had another opportunity on another ship.

By afternoon, it was apparent that we had a lot more naval personnel on board the Kempthorne than yesterday. Several hundred from the Nabob, including Fleet Air Arm personnel, were now with us. The Nabob had successfully divested itself of much of its crew that were not indispensable, and we heard two hundred or more had gone to the HMCS Algonquin. We also heard that because they had discovered significant reserves that had been stored in the officer's wardroom, those on the Nabob had better food than we had. Those of us on the Kempthorne ate only hardtack, a saltless cracker made of flour and water and baked from two to four hours. It was both hard and tasteless. We usually dipped each cracker in tea to soften it before trying to eat it. At least they were plentiful, for that was all we had to eat for the remaining five days of our voyage to Scapa Flow. We were happy to have the hardtack and tea; nobody complained.

Sometime later on, Schoolie told me about what happened on the Nabob after I'd left her. They'd gotten underway about 2213, speed five knots, course 270 degrees. Everything seemed to have quieted down, but sometime after midnight Schoolie decided he'd go to the radar room. Almost immediately he noticed a surface blip about twenty miles behind us. He watched it for a while and it became clear that it was not only following us but was gaining. At 0250, the sub was only a mile and a half off our starboard quarter. It was only a matter of a short time before that sub would be ready for another go at us. All of them, including Bobby, huddled, tense. The captain said that we had to do something about this or we'd be a dead duck.

Schoolie wondered why they just didn't detach one of the destroyers to look after the problem.

But Bobby offered to fly off and at least keep the sub down for three hours or so. If the captain changed the course in those hours, we could escape.

Everyone agreed. The decision was made. Bobby and Jupp and their crews would take off.

Because of the attitude of the flight deck, the only possible way to launch an aircraft was by using the catapult. Gus Airey, the officer in charge of that piece of machinery, wasn't sure if it would work.

The forward elevator was operative and the flight deck crew did a remarkable bit of maneuvering to bring both Bobby's and then Jupp's aircraft up from the hangar deck using the forward elevator and position them in turn on the catapult.

Schoolie held his breath. And then it happened. Bobby and his crew were airborne. The catapult had worked. Don Jupp soon followed. Both of them quickly turned and flew back toward the sub. The submarine had been cruising on the surface, but when their outlooks saw our planes bearing down on them, it crash dived. Unfortunately, the depth charges Bobby and Don Jupp were carrying had acoustic capabilities, so they couldn't drop them on the subs lest they hone on the Nabob.

While the sub was underwater, Captain Lay ordered a major change of course. Three to four hours later, when the two planes had to discontinue their watch, the submarine had been left miles behind.

Jupp was the first to come back and he made a perfect landing, taxied forward of the barrier. All of the crew got out and walked well away. That was a good thing, because Bobby forgot until too late that the stern was depressed, so his tail was too high to catch an arrestor wire, causing him to fly into the barrier. His aircraft then fell over onto Jupp's, essentially destroying it. Fortunately, nobody was hurt. The circumstances being what they were, it was necessary to get rid of the two planes, so the crew pushed them over the side into the Arctic waters.

Schoolie had watched all this with Pete Westover, a pilot, and Bill Reeks, his observer. They were a third crew standing by, on an if-needed basis. The whole event was quite an extraordinary sight to see.

I was glad that Schoolie had gone to the radar room when he had and had recognized what that blip would mean.

All the Carly Floats had been lost when the captain had given the prepare to abandon ship order. So the first thing to be done was to get enough life-saving rafts to provide for even the reduced numbers that remained on board. This is when Walter Rice took over. First, he had the men in the aircraft equipment room remove the three-man rafts stowed on board each of the remaining Avengers and brought them to the flight deck, but when he saw there were only eleven rafts, he told the equipment room men to look for spares that might have been stashed away. There they found another twenty-six three-man rafts, had them inflated, and lashed all of them to the arrestor wires on the flight deck to prevent any waves washing them overboard. These, together with some inflated large rubber tubes and several of the Nabob's boats, represented the way to continue living for those who remained, should Nabob finally succumb.

Walter already had done an extraordinary job, but there were still not enough floats for the number of crew left on board. So Walter went to see the captain and told him told him that it was necessary to divest even more of the crew. So the next day, many of the remaining crew were transferred to the HMCS Algonquin, the Kempthorne, and some other ships in the area.

I thanked Schoolie for telling me all this, none of which I would have otherwise known. For me the remaining days of our journey on the Kempthorne to Scapa Flow went quite smoothly. Time just passed checking our patients and talking with my tiffies and members of the squadron. I didn't really feel like reading any of the books in the captain's day cabin. One time "action stations" sounded and the crew of the Kempthorne sprang to action. We heard that one time they had a sonar bearing on a submarine. I found it exciting to watch as this very efficient crew went into action and fire depth charges. Plumes of water rose high in the sky. Someone said that the target had turned out to be a whale. Then for two days, we had gale force winds, during which we worried whether the Nabob could stand up to them, but she seemed to handle them with ease. On the Nabob, I'd never been seasick, but when the gales began I wondered if my good luck would continue. It did. Actually, I found the quicker and more abrupt movements of the smaller ship more pleasant than the longer roll that I'd known on the Nabob.

I spent some time on the bridge of the Kempthorne, doing little more than watching the sea, the other ships that were with us and the Catalina flying boat that escorted us day after day. Always there was the captain, Lieutenant Commander Alan Brown, R.N., sitting in what I assumed was the captain's chair, smoking his pipe, relaxed and taciturn. Neither of us ever initiated more than a superficial conversation. I did enjoy the use of his day cabin, and I made sure he knew that.

Shortly after 0800 on 27 August, we followed the Nabob into Scapa Flow, after a voyage of about 1100 miles. As we did, I realized how lucky we'd been to be only the second ship of our type that had been torpedoed and have had more than ten survivors.

Those of us who had travelled on the Kempthorne were soon ashore. There was something very substantial about standing on dry land once again. As a matter of fact, our group all kneeled and quickly kissed the earth of Scapa Flow. I made a comment, undoubtedly not original, "the more firma, the less terra," that seemed appropriate at the moment.

Soon after we were back on the Nabob, where it seemed much the same as when I'd left it. Almost immediately I met Schoolie in our cabin. There we both received notes telling us we were to go on leave immediately and that we were to take all of our possessions with us. I started to pack my steamer trunk with all the items I brought with me. As I didn't have much to pack, this did not take long. The loaded steamer trunk was relatively light, and I could pull it easily, but it did require a second person to carry it. Schoolie got all of his things together too, and off we went, first to shore and then by ferry to Thurso on the Scottish mainland.

Four of us officers travelled together, which worked out well for all involved. We located a compartment on the train, but when we learned there were to be two trains, we didn't know which train to put our luggage on. However, as they were both going via Inverness, it didn't matter. In a few minutes our train started, but for all of us sleep was difficult to achieve sitting up in the compartment's seats. We were all still very much on edge. Sometime in the early hours, the train made some sort of a noise as it crossed on a trestle and, whatever the noise was, it launched us all back to the moment the torpedo had struck. In a flash, we were all out of our seats and standing in the corridor beside our compartment, feeling a little embarrassed because we'd panicked.

On arrival at Waverly station in Edinburgh, we went immediately to the nearest hotel, the posh North British in the same building as the station. Those working at the reception desk seemed quite uninterested in four physically and emotionally exhausted, scruffy, and unwashed Canadian naval officers. Finally, a clerk said in a curt, cold voice, "We have no rooms," and abruptly turned his attention to others who were waiting. We felt snubbed, not worthy of this hotel's attention. To hell with them!

Annoyed by this unfriendly treatment, we walked across Princes Street and found the Royal British Hotel. Here the atmosphere was entirely different. Obviously, it wasn't as snooty of a hotel and we had to walk up a long flight of stairs to get to the reception area, but there with great relief I heard, "We don't have any rooms at the moment, but we will have two double rooms at eleven." The tone of the voice intimated an empathetic person.

"Wonderful," I said, "but what do you suggest we do until then?"

The clerk suggested that we could have breakfast in the dining room or go to the cinema. The movies *Saved from the Sea* and *Lifeboat* were playing.

Unanimously, we decided just to have breakfast.

Although we never at any time said anything about the Nabob, I had the feeling right from the beginning that those working at the reception desk had sensed that we had been through some type of a physical and emotional turmoil and treated us with special understanding.

Even before the appointed time, we were able to get in our rooms. How good those showers and the clean clothes we'd brought with us felt. Nor did it take us long to find the bar and enjoy some of its liquid offerings. Then we lunched and slept until the bar re-opened at five. We had dinner and entertained ourselves and others in the bar until at ten, when "Time, Gentlemen Please, Time," or the Scottish equivalent was announced, and so to bed. This quickly became our daily routine for the three remaining days we were at the Royal British, lots of sleep and lots of entertaining in the bar. None of us were interested in the sights of Edinburgh. We didn't even leave the hotel until the very last night when Schoolie and I went for a short walk on Princes Street. We just were not interested in seeing things. We were intent on being with others who were alive, convivial, and having fun. Much as at the Officers Club in Liverpool, we invited anyone who came in alone, to join us and bought them drinks. Most of the uniformed officers in Edinburgh, both men and women, were on leave and looking for rest, fun, and relaxation. Each evening those at our tables grew in number at both of our tables. Then we sub-divided and sub-divided again; one time we had four tables. All the tabs were on the two of us. The last night I had seventeen people at my table. Among them was a Norwegian pilot who had become an officer in the Royal Air Force. It turned out he was the pilot of one of the Catalina flying boats that had escorted us on much of our trip back to Scapa Flow. I made sure his cups were full.

On the fifth day, Schoolie and I set out by train for Glasgow and on to Gourock. There our destination was the Bay Hotel, which we'd come to know over the past-few months. This hotel was modest in size but quite modern and managed by a woman who was known as Two Ton Tessie, (Jean Cook), a woman of average height but considerably above average weight. Her first question was, as it always had been every time I'd checked in: "How long are you going to stay?" followed by "I want to get you on rates," which were a significant amount less than daily rate. She was as a welcoming a person to us Canadians as one could imagine. The story I'd heard was that early in the war she'd had a love affair with a Canadian naval officer, who after only a few months was lost at sea. From that time on, she'd made a point of looking after Canadian naval officers as if there was no tomorrow.

I'd stayed there for short periods several times in July, so I knew what to expect, but this time was different, for at 0900 the next morning a knock on my door awakened me. It was the chamber maid, a pleasant looking woman, whom I judged to be late middle aged. Schoolie was already up and away. She entered the room, as if to get a better look at me, and then said in a very caring voice, "Oh, you poor dear, you look so tired. May I bring you your breakfast?"

That sounded like a good idea to me and I had no trouble agreeing. She left, and I went back to sleep.

About half an hour later she re-appeared with a full breakfast that I thoroughly enjoyed. Soon, I found myself going back to sleep.

At 1200, the maid woke me up again. She was about to pick up my dirty dishes, when she took another look at me and again said, "Oh my, you still look so tired. May I bring you your lunch?" I had no objection to that, and in a half hour a full lunch arrived.

At 1530 she was back again, and she offered to draw me a bath.

I gratefully accepted, and asked her to tell me about herself. She told me that she and her husband had lived in Canada for some years, but after he died, she returned to Scotland to be with her children. But she loved Canadians.

I'd finished my bath and was dressed when Schoolie returned at about 1700. That meant the bar was open, so we went down there to see what was going on. There wasn't much happening, but Two Ton Tessie arrived, and she had plans. We were lucky tonight, she told us. It was the twelfth anniversary of one of the directors of the hotel and so there was going to be a dinner party that no one would want to miss. And they want us both to come.

The party began almost before she finished talking. Suddenly, the guests were surrounding us, none of whose name I even attempted to remember, all very pleasant, all very chatty about nothing in particular. The food was remarkable, all sorts of foods that were either difficult or impossible to find. I hadn't seen lobsters since I'd left home. We had oysters on the half shell, tenderloin steaks, all sorts of green vegetables, and desserts, tarts, ice cream, just to name a few. All of this was accompanied by appropriate wines, liqueurs and, of course, malt scotch whiskeys, which I had never before had more than tasted.

When the hour was just later than midnight, a woman's voice invited us to her house to have breakfast. It was not that far away, and she had everything ready to go. The 'somebody' was a vigorous, attractive, white-haired woman of around fifty, with a husband in a wheelchair, said to be a paraplegic. She seemed to be entirely sober, but I'd been watching her, and I was sure she must have drunk a whole fifth of whisky that evening and, now at her home, even more. I asked her how she did it and she replied, "It's been a long war and a lot of parties. It just takes practice."

I watched the breakfast being prepared. On the top of a very large stove were three large frying pans: one contained bacon, one contained eggs and one contained halved tomatoes. All of these items were said to be very difficult to obtain, but obviously, as with the dinner, everything was available in wartime Scotland, if you knew the right people or had the right connections. In due course, the party came to an end and someone drove Schoolie and me back to the Bay.

The next morning Schoolie and I went to nearby Greenock, a somewhat larger city than Gourock and where the HMCS Niobe was located. This was the major Canadian naval base in Scotland, and it was there that we went to renew our financial resources and to get any on-going news. The news for us was that the Nabob was at a buoy in the Firth of Forth, opposite Rosyth, and that we were to rejoin her forthwith.

Chapter Twenty-One

The Nabob Song

Approaching the Nabob on the boat that we took from the shore, we could see that she still had the list to starboard, but the stern was a little higher than immediately after the torpedoing. Schoolie explained that it was probably because she no longer had those big five-inch guns that were on her stern. He'd watched the crew get rid of them on the way down to Scapa.

Going on board, we were at once aware of a very pungent, heavy, slightly sweet odor, a little like vomit, and that to me even seemed to have a slight yellow colour, if an odor could have a colour. We knew at once its source, the bodies of our sea mates, still entombed in the rum locker. Knowing this made this odor (once smelled, never forgotten) even more difficult to cope with. The next day there was a ventilation system that expelled most of the odor from the ship, except when the wind direction changed, or when the ship's list changed from starboard to port with the tide. That brought the odor back temporarily in full force. Of course, living with it hour after hour led us to accommodate to it. It was the way it was and nothing more could be done to make it more tolerable, so we adapted to it.

Now that we no longer had the 340 members of 852 Squadron with us, and most of our crew had gone elsewhere, there were many, many fewer men around; this was especially noticeable in the wardroom. Apparently, the powers that be had decided to disembark all possible stores, so this activity went on from morning to night, day after day. It included such things as all the removable instruments in the Asdic and catapult compartment, laundry equipment, the aft elevator machinery and essentially everything and anything movable. In addition, in order to get the Nabob into the dry dock, the trim had to be brought closer to normal, so the various oil tanks and other forward areas were flooded. Lighters were busy day after day carrying items ashore. More and more personnel, including Schoolie, also left as time went on. I, the doctor, had to stay to the end.

After a few days, Captain Lay called me to his office. "Read," he said, "I want to commend you on the way you have carried out your duties, especially on the day we were torpedoed. You did exceptionally well; but of course, that was in line with your job, so I'm not recommending you for a medal."

I'd never even thought of a medal. I'd thought I'd just done what I was supposed to do and I wasn't especially proud of my efforts.

"Thank you, sir,"

With that, he got up from his chair, as did I. Meeting over.

My sick bay activities were routine as was life in the ward room. There, I missed Chizzy's ever-present smile and good humor. I wondered about the payment for all the liquor I'd bought for the wardroom in Edinburgh. I was told not to worry, so I didn't.

A small group of us officers and men got together almost every day to play cards and talk. For fun, one time we accumulated as many of the verses of the Fleet Air Song (A25) as we could. We found thirty-three verses, but there may be more.

Another time a small group of us enjoyed writing a parody of the then popular song *Mairsy Doats*. We called it the *The Nabob Song*. The words are as follows:

> Verse:
> When the ships going down and you think you're going to drown,
> Don't get in a panic,
> Just be like Joe,
> Go down below and pack your bag and hammock.
>
> Chorus:
> Motor boats and Carly floats and little rubble dinghies,
> Paddle your own canoe, wouldn't you?
> Paddle your own canoe, wouldn't you?

Finally, the tugs warped the Nabob alongside the wharf. I knew that this meant I would soon be leaving her, and so I went to my cabin to have a shower and get appropriately dressed. Just as I was just starting to put on my trousers, out of the blue there was the sound of what I thought was a huge explosion. It was so like the tremendous noise that accompanied our torpedoing. Instinctively, I darted out the door and bumped into one of the workmen. He assured me that there was no need to worry. They'd just dropped four hundred tons of pig iron on the steel deck just in front of my cabin. There was only a thin steel bulkhead standing between where they dropped it and my cabin, so it stood to reason that it had shaken me. He apologized, as they'd not known anyone was so close.

The explanation was simple. They'd needed to level the Nabob just a little more, so she could be brought into the dry dock. I soon recovered and finished getting ready to leave. I noticed a large cartoon one of our pilots had drawn, "The Harry Tarpon Club," hanging on the bulkhead in the wardroom. It's too good to leave behind, I thought, so I rescued it and carefully filed it away in my kit.

Not long after that, the Nabob, now virtually horizontal, was warped into the dry dock. It was then I walked across the quarter deck with my gear, about to leave the ship. There, standing on the very aft end of Nabob, was a man carefully recording each broom and each mop that was now being removed from the ship. This careful accounting of these minor items that were being saved contrasted to the way the exorbitantly expensive equipment had been tossed over the side not that long ago.

As I made that step to the shore on 28 September, one of the last to leave the ship, I felt that this dismantled ship was no longer the Nabob that I'd known, and I was relieved that these last few weeks were finally over. It was then I realized that probably I was no longer going to actively participate in stopping Hitler. As that was the very reason I'd joined up, I was very disappointed it was over, especially since the work was not yet done.

However, I'd had a role. I'd ensured the safety of the crew through my inspections, I'd treated many sailors aboard the Kempthorne, I'd brought good booze aboard the ship, and I'd saved Gavin Waite and Don Cash. In the dark moments when our lives were at risk, I'd remained calm and had done my duty as best as I could.

I'd had wonderful experiences aboard this ship, the first ever Canadian-manned aircraft carrier. I'd flown with one of the finest squadron leaders in the war. I'd met and worked alongside truly remarkable men, both officers and men. I'd said goodbye to many of the same. I would carry this with me for the rest of the life, the good and the bad.

That being settled in my mind, I began to focus on going back home to my wife and family and whatever might lie ahead.

Addendum

Shortly after I arrived back in Canada, I had a meeting in Ottawa with Mr. John Connolly, the executive assistant to the Naval Minister, the Honorable Angus MacDonald, Captain Rollo Mainguy, the Chief of Naval Personnel, and a third man whose name I do not remember and who said nothing at the meeting. I recounted what Walter and I had observed of Captain Lay's relationship with the crew and the various decisions he'd made, especially issuing the nonsensical order to prepare to abandon ship shortly after we were torpedoed and how it could have led to a disastrous loss of life because it led to the loss of most of our life preservers. I described how the captain used the life rafts from the airplanes in order to play golf and had not arranged to replace them. I also explained how he'd used poor judgment when he charged our sick berth attendant with an offense punishable by death for a minor misdemeanor. I told them how he'd forced air crew to fly when the weather was at best unfavorable and despite the advice of the squadron leader, an order which led to the loss of life. I described how he'd left a buoy ten minutes early and then threatened his senior medical officer with a court martial, as well as several other examples of poor judgment. On the positive side, I also pointed out that he had accumulated a large supply of lumber on board, undoubtedly a major element in the Nabob's survival.

At the conclusion, Captain Mainguy stated, "Be assured that as long as I hold this position, Captain Lay will never again have a command of more than ten men."

With that the meeting concluded. I felt that I had conveyed to this group most of the facts that Walter and I had previously discussed and that I thought that the naval authorities needed to know.

Afterword

Our father was a remarkable man. In fact, many times throughout our combined lives, someone always had a remark or story to be told about Charles Read.

It could have been about his days at Acadia University or his performance in plays at McGill; or perhaps about shared experiences during World War II. Many accolades emanated from his long and admirable career at the University of Iowa Hospitals and Clinics. And certainly, there have been many tales told to us about his days on the beach, on the tennis court, out fishing or partying in Prince Edward Island; a place he so loved to go every summer to rejuvenate.

Dad loved a challenging conversation and a good party—all at the same time. Life is meant to be lived to the fullest each day; he reminded us regularly. He believed in making the world a better place and he lead his life this way.

A man of principle and one true to his word, he followed through on pursuing ideas, changing ways of thinking or acting on societal aspects which bothered him. Perhaps it was that deep dark night of August 1944 when hanging off the edge of the HMS Nabob or going down below, after being torpedoed, was the beginning of this all.

Upon returning to Canada near the end of the war, our father opened a part time country practice in Prince Edward Island for several months. Many of his experiences during this time were recorded in his published book, "This Navy Doctor Came Ashore". After being discharged from the Navy in 1946, he began a residency in Pediatrics in the Montreal Children's Hospital and in his second year, he became a Medical Fellow at the Royal Victoria Hospital in Montreal. Upon completing his residency, he did a clinical research fellowship at Massachusetts General Hospital, Harvard University. In 1951, he moved to Winnipeg to be Associate Professor at the Children's Hospital. It was during this time that he learned that the diet for both the diabetic children and their parents was very difficult to follow even though this diet seemed to be the standard and no one questioned it.

Seeing that it was not scientifically based, he developed a new one which he named the "Constant Carbohydrate Diet." This diet was enthusiastically endorsed by many dieticians and became the prototype of all diets for diabetics.

In 1954, he relocated to Iowa City to join the Pediatric faculty at the University of Iowa Hospitals and Clinics as a Pediatric Endocrinologist. For about fifteen years, besides having an active clinical practice, he did extensive medical research including: development of the first method to measure growth hormone; the treatment of over-active thyroid disease in those under the age of twenty; and the development of insulin assay to more accurately measure insulin levels. By 1965, he became very interested in the role of lipids causing atherosclerosis. His recommendation to limit the fat content of diet to 30 percent led to much research in the following years.

In the late 60's he closed down his laboratory and focused on his clinical practice. In 1971, a junior medical student came to talk to him about starting a Free Medical Clinic to serve those in the community who were not receiving medical care; largely due to limited funds. Recruiting people to serve was not a problem; medical students, lab techs, nurses, residents, and pharmacists signed up. The Free Medical Clinic has grown over the years and continues to serve the medically underserved in Iowa City.

Upon retirement, our dad traveled extensively throughout the world and returned to a hobby he had as a child; photography. His art has been displayed on the walls throughout the University of Iowa including the University of Iowa Hospitals and Clinics.

Names of Children who wrote this

Charles H. Read, III
Patricia Read Botthof
Judy Read Guernsey
Susan E. Read
Connie Read Hippee

Acknowledgments

From Patricia Read Botthof:

To his dear friends and the many people who supported him over the years in a so many ways; thank you. You know who you are.

To his dear friend Alastair Currie - his greatest friend—with whom he found instant kinship which lasted to the end of both of their lives and to dear Jeanne, Alastair's life partner and Dad's steadfast friend, thank you. Alastair's and Jeanne's family has meant so much to him and our entire clan.

To our amazing mother Anne Greig Read who endured so much from a man whom she loved and from whom we have learned the true mean of grace; we love you, admire you and miss you so much.

Lastly to Chunghi, who enriched his life in so many ways over these past 40 years—and who was by his side to the end—our love and gratitude to you.

From Dr. Read:

I am especially grateful to James McKean, MFA, PhD, whose advice and suggestions were important and made the writing of this book a pleasure. Also I am grateful to Gail McClure for her extensive editing. I am also grateful to Jeremy Lammi of Lammi Publishing, Inc. for taking on this project, and to Karen Hann for her work editing the final text.

About Lammi Publishing, Inc.

Incorporated in 2014, Lammi Publishing is dedicated to publishing Canadian military history from the wars before confederation to the mission in Afghanistan. Our philosophy is that we cannot forget. Our mission is to be a method of remembrance. Canadian military history has shaped not only our politics and government, but our society as well. Canadians naturally take pride in our famous victories in Western Europe, Afghanistan and South Africa. From the oceans to the air, Canadians have done their duty with skill and valor. Peacekeeping operations have taken our forces far and wide bringing hope and security to so many. Canadian uniforms have been seen around the world as harbingers of liberation, from Belgium in WWI to the Netherlands in WWII to Yugoslavia in the 1990s.

It is only by having easy access to material on these events that we can understand them, put them in context and remember. Information, analysis, and the memoires of those who served should be readily available instead of being locked away in a desk or a long-forgotten bookcase in the back of a library.

The rise of electronic books means that it is now possible for anyone to easily compile a library that would rival the best that our public libraries or universities can offer, with no more worries about short print runs and the vagaries of the antiquarian market.

To learn more about us and what we are doing, check out our website.
http://lammipublishing.ca

Printed in Poland
by Amazon Fulfillment
Poland Sp. z o.o., Wrocław

59091193R00103